NINE PRINCIPLES FOR INSPIRED ACTION:

A NEW & TARGETED PERSPECTIVE

Ronald Finklestein
With Robert Schepens

FOREWORD
Tony Rubleski

NINE PRINCIPLES FOR INSPIRED ACTION!
A NEW & TARGETED PERSPECTIVE

By Ron Finklestein
With Robert Schepens
© 2009. All Rights Reserved

ISBN: 978-0-9760297-0-0

Published by:

Published by AKRIS INC
211 Harcourt Dr.
Akron, Ohio 44313
info@akris.netwww.akris.net

Cover & Interior Design By:

R E L E V ∧ N T
branding. marketing. advertising.

297 Clay Ave. Suite 105
Muskegon, MI 49440
(231) 799-4949
www.RelevantMethod.com

ENDORSEMENTS

"Ron's "Nine Principles" solves the mystery and cracks the true success code through the experience, successes, and failures of his own business and those of his clients. His proven formula allows you to break free of the confusion experienced by so many entrepreneurs seeking a "magic pill" to greatness, and provides you the roadmap to lasting success in both business and life."

Steve Underation, Best Selling Author of *Trade Show Profit Secrets,* **co-author of** *The Platinum Rule for Trade Show Mastery*
www.tradeshowprofitsystems.com

"There is a formula to achieve anything ... family, sports, business ... anything. In Taking Inspired Action, Ron clearly sets forth the formula for overall personal and professional success that anyone can achieve."

Frank Agin, Author
Foundational Networking

"The principles in this book matched my own beliefs including taking 100 percent responsibility for our lives, discovering what we are meant to do (innermost passions) and taking inspired actions that ultimately fulfill our innermost needs and those of others simply because we are totally on purpose with our life. If you want to learn the secrets of super successful people, this book will re-awaken dormant knowledge buried deeply within you!"

Stephen Hopson, Former Award-Winning Wall Street Stockbroker turned Inspirational Speaker, Writer and first deaf pilot in the world with an instrument rating

"A plan without action is only a DREAM! In his new book "Nine Principles" Ron Finklestein explains the power of taking personal ownership and appropriate action to achieve what you want in business and life. I call this being "above the line." Ron's first principle of intelligent self-interest is a key ingredient. Unfortunately, it is often misunderstood and ultimately blocks our journey to success. The "Nine Principles" creates a pathway that leads us to continuous learning, growth and to becoming the truly successful person we know we can be. Read this book!"

Ralph Berge, Business Coach and Owner of Action Coach of the North Coast

"Ron has gone beyond personal development. His unique insight into human behavior allows you to go to your core to not only better understand yourself, but those you communicate with in business. What I love about Ron Finklestein's writing is that he not only identifies the problem, but gives you the common sense answer with a fresh approach to have greater success."

Dale Stefancic, Radio Personality
EntrepreneursonCall.com

"I live my life by these principles! I had Ron create a poster listing these principles that I put on my office wall to remind myself daily how to grow a profitable business!"

Litsa Voulgaris, Aris Financial Services
My revenues have improved by more than 50%.
Dave Vespoli, Financial Planner

"I got one hour a day back by implementing these concepts in my life."

D.A. Stauffer, Stauffer Patent Services LLC

"I have totally changed how I think about my business and my life. These principles are truly empowering."

Maureen Gechter, Probate Attorney

"For over four years I have actively participated in a group using these principles. The value is incalculable and the opportunities for focused personal and professional growth are the most effective I've encountered in over ten years."

Alan L. Plastow, MAT, PMP
Founder, The Business Technology Consumer Network and The Institute for Technology Asset Management, Co-Founder, Charter Member, The Consortium for Technology Portfolio Management Excellence @Kent State University

"I continue to grow both personally and professionally using these principles. They are simple and effective."

Don Philabaum, Internet Strategies Group.
Author of Internet Dough

V

"Ron Finklestein knows what makes winners win! Through a combination of personal experience and keen observation, he has identified the nine specific behaviors that lead successful people to succeed. In Taking Inspired Action... Ron shows you how consistently and "selfishly" applying these behaviors will drive success in business and in life. There's no magic here - just simple, practical and powerful insights that, when mastered, can transform you into a peak performer at those critical "moments of truth" that define the difference between failure and success."

Carl Rakich, CEO/Head Coach, The Coach Zone, LLC

VI

ACKNOWLEDGEMENTS

Any book of this magnitude requires the effort of many people. There are too many to list here but I want to acknowledge those who took the time to read the manuscript and provide feedback; the mastermind group who challenged me on the very concept that went into this book. This group included: David Akers, Stephen Brand, Joe Smucny, Jeff Nischwitz, Al Plastow, and Seth Briskin.

To Ron McDaniel of Buzzoodle, who gladly assumed the awesome responsibility of being my accountability partner, to ensure this book was written in a timely manner. Thanks Ron.

To Litsa Vouglaris, who made me understand how impactful this book could be. This became clear when she shared with me her experience in reading a draft of this book and she questioned her assumptions behind what she did. Thanks Litsa.

A special thanks to Shauna M. Kaminsky and Mary Helsel who, after reading the book, shared their thoughts with me, leading to the book's title.

A special thanks to Tshombé N. Brown, Charity Beall, John Joyce, Dan Konfal and Carol Hayden for feedback on the chapter on Selfishness (intelligent self-interest).

To my friends at AM Akron Toastmasters, who provided valuable feedback on the contents of this book, either by reading the manuscript or listening to the contents through the many speeches I gave as I tested the material.

To all the members of my Business Mastery Advisory Boards(tm) who freely shared with me their thoughts and dreams, goals and aspirations, challenges and opportunities, and kept an open mind about transforming their business and their life.

DEDICATION

To my wife Sheila and our children, Aaron and Emily; without you there would be no book nor would I be the person I am today. Thank you!

AND

Robert Schepens, my friend and mentor, who encouraged me to follow my dream and write this book. Bob gave freely of his time, energy, and knowledge to help create this book. His probing questions, relentless pursuit for knowledge, and challenging feedback helped me grow both as a person and a businessman. Thank you!

HOW TO READ THIS BOOK

As people read this book prior to publication, I received three types of responses to this material:

1. "I cannot and will not do what you suggest in this book. I only read this book because I know you."

2. "You mean I am allowed to be selfish?"

3. "Why are you talking about this? It is obvious and it is not new."

By far, most of the feedback came from items one and two above.

"I cannot and will not do what you suggest."

The content of this book sometimes flies in the face of accepted cultural norms. When I ask you to get really focused on your intelligent self-interest, to get selfish, it is through this selfishness that greatness occurs, however we define our greatness. Please do not pass judgment on this material and keep an open mind as you read.

All great achievement comes not from reason but from emotion. I once heard Dan Clark describe it this way: "Reason leads to conclusions, emotions lead to action." It is hard to take action, especially inspired action, if you do not care deeply about something. You cannot focus your limited time, energy and money unless it is very important to you. It is OK to care deeply, to the exclusion of things that do not support your intelligent self-interest. It is about taking action on things that are important to you and knowing, deep in your heart, you are doing the right things, taking inspired action.

That is how this book was born. I want to change the lives of millions by helping others think differently. We need to get away from any entitlement mentality we learned. We are responsible for our life and our business. Our actions need to come from us, independent from what is happening outside. This book is about helping you to think differently. I learned to think differently and saw dramatic changes in my life. I taught these principles to my clients and saw dramatic differences in their lives.

As you move forward keep in mind rule number one: Keep an open mind. Learning to think differently comes from entertaining thoughts and ideas that are not consistent with your existing beliefs. Some of you will find this book a difficult read. If this is case for you, use your pen or highlighter to mark the concepts that are difficult and think about them. Why do you react so strongly to these concepts? You may choose not to embrace them but at least you questioned your beliefs and strengthened your intelligent self-interest and that is good.

Some of you will read this book and say to yourself "I am allowed to be selfish?"

Yes, you are allowed. This comment is what really inspired me to complete this book. It was by far the most frequent comment.

We are taught from the time we born not to be selfish: "share your toys" or "don't be selfish." I would agree with this perspective if it is not being motivated and driven by your intelligent self-interest. True unselfishness comes from being totally and completely selfish. As adults we have only so much time, energy, money and resources. If we have big plans we must be selective in sharing, otherwise we can do great harm in achieving our goals.

So rule number two is simple. It is ok to say "no," especially when you have a clear vision of what you want to achieve. If your action does not take you where you want to go, why are you doing it?

For experienced achievers, they already know this material and asked me why I chose to write about it. "Why are you talking about this? It is obvious and it is not new." What they forget is that they learned it somewhere. If you already know this material, read this book so you can consciously know what you are doing right. Read this book so you can teach your children, employees and other important people in your life about creating success through inspired action. Give the book away to someone who can benefit for this material if you do not have the time to teach it.

Finally, rule number three, if you know this material, use it as a reminder to yourself to keep doing what you are doing and keep doing it. If you know it and you are not doing it, then decide now to take inspired action by creating your intelligent self-interest.

TABLE OF CONTENTS

Self-Interest to take ownership? How does ownership lead to effectiveness? Why results, not accomplishments, are important.

You know what results you want, how do you get them? Why measurable, repeatable and predictable are critical to your success. How do you teach others the way you want things done?

Success is about inspiring others to take action. Why your success dependent on others and what can you do?

Why mistakes are essential to your success. How do you fail forward? Why do you want to fail forward?

Keeping yourself focused is asking three questions.

Why too many ideas are not good. Why the wrong ideas are harmful to your intelligent self-interest. How do you determine a good idea when you see one?

Redefining success. Why this new definition is critical. How does this definition apply to you?

Foreword By Tony Rubleski, President - Mind Capture Group

When a person reveals their story and wisdom you're best served to notice, listen and learn from their experiences both good and bad. Ron's new book opens up with his own challenges and victories throughout his business life and the growing process he's seen within not only himself, but his clients and the people closest to him. This takes guts but it builds an immediate bridge of authenticity in a world crowded with misguided advice givers.

His new book is direct and full of sage advice from the frontlines. Ron takes us into client case studies to prove his points and make his case for the powerful strategies contained within this hard hitting, and concisely written book. I read a lot of books and I can quickly sniff out theory from 'real world' application and I'm pleased to let you know that Ron delivers the goods with his latest book.

Many of the challenges I see with my marketing clients are the same ones Ron describes with many of his as well. Here's the beauty of the last statement; as Tony Robbins says, *Success Leaves Clues*, which is powerful advice indeed. Ron's challenges and successes outlined during the course of this book help to save us time and improve not only our own life, but the lives of others.

This book lays out a compelling case to the power of setting and tracking goals and holding yourself accountable. In today's sped up, fragmented world, these are sadly foreign concepts to most people who want the quick-fix solution to their problems versus achieving mastery in certain key disciplines that Ron lays out in a simple, yet highly effective fashion. If you ignore these core strategies you'll often find yourself frustrated and dealing with the same recurring issues time and time again.

In a world of distraction and shortened attention spans I urge you to not only read this book but chunk it down, as Jack Canfield would say, into simple action strategies you apply each day to help you build a better business, organization and life for not only yourself but those around you.

Chapter Six on the *Power of Persistence* is well worth the investment of time and money in reading Ron's book. By describing the mindset of champions and how to deal with criticism, he gives you ammunition to improve your situation when criticism appears. Believe me, people who are jealous or unhappy themselves will attempt to sabotage your success, goals and dreams and you must not let them. Constructive criticism is one thing, but robbing someone of their dreams is a different story in itself. The world we live in is buried in negative information and your mission is to fight through it and apply the success strategies contained within these pages. Too many people have given up and this is a tragedy. If you know someone having a challenge, get an extra copy of the book and put a Post-it note on this chapter to inspire and help them turn their negative thoughts into positive ambition.

As you read through the book you'll pick up that Ron wants you to achieve more and each chapter lays out a logical blueprint to aid you in this mission. Knowing how challenging a book can be to craft, assemble and edit, I appreciate how he's made success more achievable for those who not only read, but more importantly implement what he says. I'd much rather study from those who've already been successful versus trying to figure it out myself and wasting valuable resources. Time is short and this book will shave off years of trial and error when applied.

I commend Ron for thanking his wife in his change from employee to entrepreneur. The old adage, *behind every great man is a great woman*, is so true and I know that the people closest to us are often the biggest believers in us even when we may not quite fully yet have 100% faith in ourselves. By sharing this about his wife it also lets you know that Ron is humble enough to understand that success is a team effort and not a solo journey.

Let this book serve as your blueprint and guide to building not only a better business, but a better life for those you *selfishly* take on the journey of business with you. Kudos to Ron for writing a timely, valuable and highly relevant book in a world seeking wisdom during a time of massive change!

Tony Rubleski
Bestselling Author, *Mind Capture* book series
www.MindCaptureBook.com

INTRODUCTION

After years of reading about a variety of self improvement and personal growth topics, from a variety of authors, I came to an amazing realization: I was not achieving my goals because I was not taking the necessary action. I did not know how to harness my limited time, energy and resources to move forward towards my selfishness (intelligent self-interest). How could I identify my intelligent self-interest, determine the actions I needed to take, and then take action?

I cofounded a business conference that afforded me the privilege of working with some very successful people. The purpose of the conference was to identify what business owners did to be successful and to have these successful business owners share their best practices with the conference attendees. As I worked on this conference, I was fortunate enough to read nominations from hundreds of businesspeople who applied for this opportunity.

Over the years I started seeing a trend. This trend showed me that all the business owners who applied performed the same nine actions. I think of them as principles for a great business.

These nine principles are:

1. Selfishness (intelligent self-interest)

2. Taking total ownership for where you are in your business and your life

3. Measuring all results and implementing what works into the business so others can take the same actions

4. Inspiring people to accept both the personal and corporate vision

5. Staying focused on what is important

6. Being disciplined on doing what works

7. Being persistent because when you implement something new your performance will suffer until you have mastered this new behavior

8. Surrounding yourself with people and resources who can help you with inspired ideas that take you deeper into your intelligent self-interest

9. Taking action

As I identified and distilled these principles into their current form, I felt the need to use these principles in my own life and with my clients. The results were incredible. My clients got clear on what was important to them (intelligent self-interest) and how the business they were building would help them create their ideal life. In one case a business owner realized he did not like being a business owner with employees. As he explored his intelligent self-interest he realized he liked consulting and creating new products. He sold his business and started a new consulting firm that allowed him to follow his intelligent self-interest. In my own business I focused my entire business on teaching, coaching and implementing these principles.

Why are these principles so important? Einstein said, "We cannot solve problems by using the same kind of thinking we used when we created them." As a result, many of the challenges we experience can be remedied by changing our thinking. Once we change our thinking we can see things differently. Once we see things differently, we can determine a course of action that may not have been available to us before.

Let us look at some concepts that will help you to think differently. Let's focus on the first problem: our beliefs. I have found that our belief system is the biggest obstacle holding us back. Our beliefs are our evaluation of something. Frequently when we re-evaluate a situation, our belief about that situation will change. If your beliefs are holding you back, you must change them.

Many times our success is hindered not because we don't know what to do but by behaviors that sabotage our success. As children we grew up with beliefs that we freely accepted. These beliefs came from our parents, clergy, teachers and other important people in our lives at the time. We watched how they behaved and saw the results they achieved (or not), and somewhere along the way we thought emulating those behaviors was in our best interest. Many of us made decisions as children, based on our limited experience, that we still hold today.

Why is that a problem? Because most of us do not know what we believe, and we have accepted beliefs that may not be in our best interest. An example might help.

I was teaching a class on dealing with difficult people. One lady in the room was very outgoing and she wore her emotions on her sleeve. Her supervisor asked her to attend because they were experiencing some personal conflict at work. Her problem: she became very angry when her supervisor asked her to calm down. During class, as she shared her story, I asked her why she became upset when her supervisor asked her to calm down.

Her response: "Because my mother always told me that and I hated it then and I hate it now."

My response: "So you are responding to your supervisor the same way you respond to your mother?"

Her response: Silence.

She did not realize this dynamic was in her life. She believed that the only way to deal with someone asking her to calm down was to react to others the same way she reacted to her mother. She did not realize she had a choice. Just by seeing how she reacted to her supervisor, she was able to choose how she would react to her supervisor.

What beliefs are you carrying around about money, people, success, religion, etc. that are hindering your success? Inherent in limiting beliefs is the core of new opportunity. If you are reading this book, you must understand that you can choose what you want to believe and take substantial action in moving toward your intelligent self-interest. **We want you to focus on what you want, what is important to you, not on what you don't want.**

Using our above example, we could change the question and stop working on why this woman was creating a bad relationship with her supervisor. Instead, we could ask what kind of relationship she wants and help her achieve the skills necessary to achieve this relationship.

Another challenge we have is the outrageously fast pace of change we are dealing with daily. Corporate security is a thing of the past. We need to ask ourselves what security means to us and create a plan to move in that direction. It is estimated that the amount of new information doubles every two years. This means if you are not constantly learning, you are putting your livelihood in jeopardy. Someone will always be there to take your job (or replace you when you stop being effective).

You must now think of yourself as self-employed, even if you work for someone else. When you treat yourself as a business owner, you will make different decisions, you will become a lifelong learner, and you will continue to acquire new skills.

Think about it this way. There are over 3000 new books published daily. Some of this is new knowledge, some is repackaging of old information, and some of it is not important. You must continue to upgrade your skill set regularly, especially when it is estimated that the amount of new information will double every 72 hours by 2015. How do you keep up? How do you keeping making yourself valuable to the organization? You can keep up by focusing on the principles in this book and spending your time, energy and money on what takes you closer to your intelligent self-interest.

Let's take a minute to discuss ownership. This is an easy principle to explain but it is hard to implement. Simply put, you must own the whole of your circumstances. This means you are 100% responsible for everything that happens in your life, even if you cannot explain it.

I once had a brain tumor. The doctors did not know what caused it but it was my problem and I could choose how I wanted to respond. I took all the necessary action (from a legal perspective) to ensure everything was taken care in the event surgery was not successful. I did not worry about what caused the tumor but I did take 100% ownership of how I handled it: the doctors, lawyers, treatment, recovery, etc. I felt I was making the correct decisions because they were choices I wanted to embrace instead of doctors, lawyer or other specialists telling me what to do.

If you can take total ownership of your situation you will experience something powerful. You will feel empowered. After all, if you own it you can change it, or at least change your attitude about it. If sales are down you can do something about it, even if it means you change your belief system about why sales are down. Many times, we as business owners blame the economy when sales are down. I hear that a lot. When I hear that, I ask my clients (or myself) why others are successful in the same economy. If they can do it I can do it as well and so can you. If you continuously are making bad decisions, you can take ownership and get professional help to make better decisions. Ownership does not mean things will suddenly get easier. It simply means you can do something about the situation. The fact that you can do something is very empowering.

One misconception is the importance of persistence. When you learn something new your performance suffers. Just watch a child learning to walk. He stands up, stumbles and sits down. Typically he will smile because it was new and exciting. He will repeatedly fall and that's ok. By falling he begins to understand what does not work. Eventually he puts everything together and takes the first step. But that is only the beginning. After that it is not long before he learns to run, ride a bike, or start skateboarding. At a young age he is passionate about learning, as you should be as well.

I've done a lot of process redesign work in my career. Through this I learned the importance of persistence. I once worked with a large Midwestern bank. A team of us redesigned the accounts payable process. Productivity was measured by the number of invoices a clerk paid daily. When we started, each clerk was paying 75 invoices per day. After the process was redesigned and implemented, the same clerks were processing 300 invoices per day per person. The strange thing is that in transitioning from the old system to the new system, productivity dropped to 25 invoices per day per person. Once the new skills were mastered, productivity rose very quickly.

Personal performance improvement happens the same way. Do you think the bank would have stopped the implementation when performance suffered during implementation? It would have been foolish to stop. They had made a significant investment in getting ready for the new system, so they needed to see it through. When you are making personal changes, keep this concept in mind.

Your personal performance is based on habits you build over a lifetime of learning. It took time to build the existing habits that you are using today. Know that when you change them, it will take some time. Give yourself that time and keep practicing the new behaviors. Be persistent. The result will come.

People are essential to our success. We need to understand that our success is 100% dependent on how well we lead, motivate, inspire, and influence others to take action. As we change our attitudes and beliefs we will scare others in our lives. Some will change with us; others will leave. It is not easy but the rewards will be exactly what you want, especially when you get clear on what is important to you. If you continue to associate with people who reinforce your negative belief systems, how can you expect to implement the changes? It just won't happen. Surround yourself with people who will support you in achieving your goals. It is hard enough changing; don't let others stop you. Ownership is the first step in learning to think differently. Knowing the role people play in making this happen is an important second step; choose the people in your life carefully.

We can have all the skills and knowledge necessary to achieve our desired outcomes. This knowledge and these skills are useless unless we take action. Action is the cornerstone of success. Most action, if unsuccessful, can be corrected by taking different action. Inaction can never be corrected, except by action.

Brian Tracy quotes these numbers. He says successful people and businesses invest 3% of revenues back into training for the purposes of creating new skills and keeping current on existing skills. He defines successful companies as those in the top 20% of their industries (by revenue) and successful individuals as those in the top 20% of their income brackets.

How much time and money do you spend on personal improvement, learning new skills and making yourself indispensable? There are many ways to acquire this knowledge: books, tapes, audio programs, online learning websites, courses, seminars, etc. One of my favorite places to learn new skills is at www.ilearningglobal.biz/ronf. If self improvement is important to you check out this website.

What is in it for you

So what's in it for you when you embrace these principles? Once you know and understand these principles, you will understand why they work. Once you start using these principles, you will experience how much more effective and productive you will be.

I created a coaching product I call the Business Mastery Advisory Board(tm) (www.rpfgroupinc.com). I asked each member of this board why they participate and what keeps them involved. Here is what they told me:

1. "I am learning to think differently!"

2. "I am growing Personally/Professionally!"

3. "I found out I am not alone. Others are dealing with the same problems!"

4. "I am helping others and solving my problems at the same time!"

I tell you this because the Business Mastery Advisory Board is designed to drive the nine behaviors discussed in this book. If it works for them it can work for you. I want to help you be more successful by learning to think differently. I want you to grow personally and professionally, and help you understand we are all dealing with the same issues. I want to share with you the same concepts and actions that allowed them to get great results.

I wrote this book from my learning and experience with the Business Mastery Advisory Board with the express intention of teaching you to think differently. We will accomplish this through the nine principles that all successful people implement. In the next nine chapters I will be discussing each of these principles.

Take a look at the people you know who are making a positive difference in your life or the lives of others. I could list the names of dozens of people you have not heard of who live their lives to a higher standard, who believe in their intelligent self-interest. They are business owners, people who join Toastmasters (public speaking), and people who learn new skills because they love to learn and share what they have learned with others.

To review, the nine principles we will discuss in this book are: intelligent self-interest or selfishness, ownership, results, people, discipline, persistence, ideas, and action. Keep an open mind as you read. After all, we want you to think differently about your situation.

Ron Finklestein
330-990-0788
www.rpfgroupinc.com
Ron@akris.net

CHAPTER 1:

THE POWER OF SELFISHNESS (INTELLIGENT SELF-INTEREST)

"The test of first-rate intelligence is the ability to hold two opposing ideas in mind at the same time, and still maintain the ability to function."

–F. Scott Fitzgerald

We are going to discuss some ideas that, at first glance, appear to oppose each other: selfishness as intelligent. The foundation for success comes from defining selfishness as intelligent self-interest. Please keep an open mind as you read this chapter before you decide whether to embrace or discard it.

Let's begin our story of a person, a real person, named Bill (not his real name). We will follow Bill as he identifies and implements these principles.

It all came to a head at 9/11/01. You see, Bill had been working as a consultant for some of the largest companies in the world. Over the past few years he became unhappy with his work. He would go in and make all kinds of changes and leave before he had a chance to see how his changes worked. At first it was fun and exciting. As time went by it got to be more and more frustrating. He would spend months in a strange city, away from his wife and kids, working 12 hours a day and not seeing the long term results of his work.

Prior to 9/11 businesses were dealing with the Year 2000 (Y2K) problem. Companies invested billions of dollars fixing the date change problems on computer systems. The problem was simple but very complex to fix. Computer systems, process control systems, copiers and faxes would read 1900 when the date changed to 1/1/2000.

Bill was working with companies to solve these problems. When business slowed the company Bill worked for offered him a 40% pay cut to stay with the company. Bill, a veteran of the job search, was not happy and felt betrayed that this company would do this. He took the meager severance package and started his job search.

Then came 9/11/2001. He knew his life was different as he watched the plane hit the second tower of the World Trade Center in New York City. He did not know how much it would change, but he did know life as he knew it was over.

Over the next year, Bill was forced to face his dissatisfaction with his work, the lack of job opportunities, and the impact this situation had on his family. He came face to face with his worst fear: there has to be more to work than this.

Bill began questioning his beliefs and his fears. He questioned what he wanted from life (he was almost 50 years old). He decided to put himself through an exercise that would help him get clear on what was important to him.

He projected himself out into the future 35 years. He was now 85. He thought that would be a good age to die. As he looked back at his life from the vantage point of an 85-year-old he realized his life had no real meaning. He had spent his life moving away from what he did not want. He found himself sad and unhappy, for he felt he had wasted his life. He was successful by the world's standards - beautiful wife, great income, wonderful children - but he still felt empty and unfulfilled.

At this point he realized he needed to make major changes. He needed to find out what he wanted to do for the rest of his life. He wanted to move forward to something meaningful. He needed to define how to go from successful to significant in the remaining days of his work life. He needed to create his intelligent self-interest. He needed to feel he was making a difference as he tackled this second career. This is Bill's story.

Bill realized he needed to think differently. What worked in his past was not working now and his first commitment to himself was to determine what would give his life meaning. He wanted to change the vision he had of himself as an 85-year-old and as he looked back over his life, he wanted to feel good about what he had done with the last 35 years. He realized this was not a long time.

He talked to his wife. He felt with the current state of the job market he would have better opportunities elsewhere. This was a problem because he had children in high school and his wife had elder parents who needed her help.

He talked with his children. One was a senior in high school and was soon to launch a life of his own. The other was a sophomore in high school and he did not want to impact her life by asking her to move. He told his daughter of his decision to move and told her she could join him after graduation. He walked away from that discussion wishing he could help her understand. That was a lot for a 16-year-old to understand.

His daughter, wanting to help, went to school and talked to the counselor. She realized if she went to summer school she could graduate a year early. She was very proud of this and she went home to tell her father of her decision.

He listen to her idea and asked her why she would give up being captain of the soccer team, membership in Character Counts, and the other activities she was involved in. She simply said, "I don't want to be away from you for two years."

This statement transformed his life. At that moment he made three decisions that put his life in focus. His first decision was to apologize to his children for putting them in such a tough situation. His second decision was "I have great skills, there is no reason I should be unemployed!" This is where he began his journey and transformed himself from an employee to a business owner. His third decision focused on changing his attitude. He decided he was tired of hearing all the negative news and he was going to do something about it. This third decision, more than the other two, transformed him and his family in a very difficult but positive way. He started a business conference to focus on what business owners did right to share best practices with other business owners to help them grow, flourish and get results. This is where Bill identified his intelligent self-interest and transformed his life.

The exercise of getting clear on your intelligent self-interest (ISI) keeps your mind in order and attracts to you the things you need to make life more enjoyable. When you train yourself in the practice of deliberately staying focused on your selfishness, you will find that your thoughts and actions proceed in a more orderly procession than ever before. In other words, when you understand your selfishness and hold it with your mind, it makes decisions easier and action clearer.

Before we go too far let's define selfishness as intelligent self-interest (ISI) and define intelligent and self-interest. Words change in meaning over time and I want to look at the words as they were introduced into the English language.

We can begin to understand that we are talking about an important and significant issue that can change our lives in a positive and meaningful way. Please understand dear reader that I am using intelligent self-interest and selfishness interchangeably. Before I can discuss the eight other principles, we must fully understand the power of intelligent self-interest.

To start building a good foundation we must define some terms so we are on the same page (no pun intended). By doing this we will clarify some issues and avoid the confusion that happens without a clear understanding of the words we use.

Intelligence

The word intelligent, according to the website www.ety-monline.com, means a "faculty of understanding," from L. *intelligentia* "understanding," from *intelligentem* (nom. *intelligens)* "discerning," prp. of *intelligere* "to understand, comprehend," from *inter-* "between" + *legere* "choose, pick out, read. "

Selfish

The word selfish comes from the word self. Self, according to the same website, means "one's own person, same." Synonyms include *self-seeking* (1628), *self-ended* and *self-ful*.

Interest

The word interest comes from *interresse*, "to concern, make a difference, be of importance." *Interesting* meant "important" (1711).

If we put these definitions together we can see that intelligent self-interest simply means: intelligent - to understand, comprehend and choose; self - self-ended or for our own self; and interest - "what's important." For our purposes, let's define intelligent self-interest as meaning that we understand, comprehend and choose what is important to us. From this definition we are to define what is important to us and choose how this is important to others.

But we can't stop there. It is too easy to abuse this concept and use it for selfish, non-intelligent purposes. Selfish indeed has come to invoke the word "outcast," when the act of denoting a person to be an outcast is in itself an act of selfishness by putting your own values above those of someone else. A conundrum to be sure; it is the "Us Versus THEM" concept.

In this book, we are attempting to define useful principles for the businessperson, or any person, in their quest for success and happiness that make sense of the life we have chosen by the goals we have defined. We use postulated derivatives of a word, "selfish," which is in itself full of dichotomies that do not allow it to become a useful principle.

Are we using the term "self-interest" to mitigate the pejorative point of view? When we add the word "intelligent" to "self-interest," are we in fact simply attempting to water down the connotation of the word "selfish" as used in today's society? I don't think so and let me tell you why.

We use the word "intelligent" in the sense of capacity to reason, to plan, to solve problems, to think abstractly, to comprehend ideas, to use language, and to learn (Wikipedia), and in so doing we assign the context of that word a less emotional or sinister import.

There is a term we CAN in fact use to do a "Ya Know What I Mean?" on the entire concept of "Intelligent Self-interest": **Intent**. We could in fact define Intelligent Self-Interest as: "Selfishness **without the intent** of being selfish." We could talk about Mother Theresa, Gandhi, Henry Ford, and Martin Luther King as prime examples of selfishness without the intent of being selfish. Mother Theresa devoted her whole life to working with the poor and indigent of Calcutta. Gandhi freed a nation through nonviolence. Henry Ford was successful in putting a car in every garage. Martin Luther King wanted to correct injustice. Each of these individuals showed intelligent self-interest (by our definition). They accomplished great things through selfishness that otherwise would not have been possible. Through their intelligent self-interest they were selfless by accomplishing great things for others.

Our use of "intelligent self-interest" is this: "Selfishness without the intent of being selfish." In this we also assume that there is an observer who can and will evaluate and judge INTENT. If the intent is malicious, the self-interest becomes selfish. If the intent is "with good will" then it becomes "intelligent" (rational, good intent). We are neither "just out for ourselves," nor are we "just out for you."

Now that we have "justified" selfishness as intelligent self-interest, we are now allowed to focus on achievements without worrying about what you may be doing **to** others.

Let's bring this discussion down to earth. This book is not designed to be a treatise on intelligent self-interest, but it is designed to help you understand that it is ok and desirable for you to focus on your intelligent self-interest.

Getting clear on your intelligent self-interest is so very important. If we use our intelligent self-interest as inspiration to accomplish great things, we have some major constraints to deal with. The first is to understand what the words "inspiration" and "great" mean. Not all of us are destined to achieve greatness, if we identify greatness as being like Oprah Winfrey, Bill Gates, or Presidents Kennedy, Lincoln, Washington; some would call that notoriety. And that is not a bad thing. Does that mean we cannot do great things if we are not famous? Of course not. It simply means we must understand what inspires greatness.

Inspiration

Inspire in this sense is c.1340, from O.Fr. *enspirer*, from L. *inspirare*, a loan-transl. of Gk. *pnein* in the Bible. The general sense of "influence or animate with an idea or purpose" is from 1390.

Great

(1538) This is from the similar use of Fr. *grand*, itself used as the equivalent of L. *magnus*, in the sense of "excellent, wonderful."

Since we now know that inspired means "influenced or animated with an idea or purpose" and greatness means "excellent, wonderful," we can begin to see why our intelligent self-interest is so important. We become inspired to greatness (and we inspire others to greatness) by our intelligent self-interest.

By greatness I am talking about the individual who takes inspired action, overcomes his fear, and reaches beyond what is expected or perceived possible. This may include starting a business, having children, overcoming cancer, or starting over in a new career. Each individual who takes inspired action has the potential for greatness and to understand their greatness.

Please notice I am talking about greatness as taking action to achieve our intelligent self-interest, nothing more or nothing less. We often confuse notoriety with greatness. They are not the same. Being famous is not the same as doing great things.

To accomplish our greatness we have to understand we have limitations. These limitations might be time, money, or other resources specific to our situation. Because it is impossible to accomplish our greatness unless we use our limited resources wisely, we must know what we want to achieve. We need to be intelligent in our use of these resources to accomplish our intelligent self-interest. Because we have so many people asking us to spend our hard-earned money, limited time and precious resources, we must be very clear on what is important to us and be very selfish about using our resources to achieve this greatness.

Stated differently, I am asking you to be focused on your intelligent self-interest. I am asking you to express this intelligent self-interest through the effective use of your of limited time, energy and money. I am asking you to take action. Your ISI will allow you to focus your time, energy and money on what you want to achieve by taking inspired action.

When you stay focused on your intelligent self-interest, obstacles tend to disappear, or if you see them, they are not as daunting as they might first appear. They become challenges to be overcome, new opportunities to be embraced, not obstacles that stop you. Taking inspired action to move forward requires you to take one step at a time, never losing sight of your end results, your intelligent self-interest.

Let us take a moment to discuss what can happen if you are not clear on your ISI. Recently, I was engaged by a client because he was unable to take action. He had so much going on in his personal life (health problems) and in his company (market changes, employee turnover, and other business opportunities he was exploring) that he was paralyzed with fear. In the past, he had made some bad business decisions and he was afraid that history would repeat itself. We talked about this and I got a good understanding of his challenges. He was successful by all standards and he had a successful company. No one could have guessed at his mental turmoil.

He lacked direction and focus and he was emotionally overextended. He did not have the same passion he had when he started his company. As he matured as a business owner, he lost his zest for the business. I gave him a simple assignment. I wanted him to be selfish and focus on his ISI. I wanted him to figure out what kind of life he wanted and how owning the business or executing any of the other opportunities would help him achieve his ISI. I then asked him to make one small decision that would move him towards his ISI. Being successful requires being selfish.

The next morning I received an email from him outlining two decisions he had made that required action. It was like a door opened for him. He decided to close his company and go to work for a large multi-national company that needed his expertise. They made him a great offer. He realized he was ready for a new challenge and when he embraced this new challenge, he became reinvigorated. Frankly, he just needed permission to pursue his ISI and make the decision he knew he wanted to make. He needed to realize that his ISI had changed and it was ok to embrace this new approach.

There are two lessons in the above story.

First, your ISI can change over time and many times it does change. I have talked with people who have been doing the same work since college. They have a hard time understanding that the decisions they made in college were good decisions at the time, but as they grow, change and mature into their ISI, what is important to them can change as well. When you leave college, your primary focus is your career. After a while you might focus on your family and their needs, and after that something else may grow in importance. Honor that need in you that wants to grow, achieve and become, the need to take inspired action.

The second lesson is that action is in fact required. Inaction can only be corrected by action. When is doubt, do something. Clarity comes from action.

What simple decision can you make to move into your intelligent self-interest? Make one decision, take one action, take that one step that moves you to your greatness, however your define it. Don't worry about how things will work out. Your purpose is to take small steps, make small decisions. Just know the universe will conspire to help you but the universe requires you to take action.

I am talking about the use of intelligent self-interest as it leads to success. Success can be defined as a fulfilling life, great and loving relationships, and abundance. The fact that success means something different to each of us can cause a problem when trying to simplify something so complex into something everyone can relate to.

Before we go too far, let us define success. Success is defined as action. This definition of success is easy to understand and I devote a whole chapter to this concept later in the book. But first I want you to understand that selfishness is a great idea which should be embraced and developed in your life. After you get clear on your selfishness, you can take inspired action to achieve your intelligent self-interest. The result of action is success, the outcomes you have worked so hard to achieve.

The best way to describe this type of intelligent self-interest is with a true story.

One business owner I met fell on some hard times. The hard times were the direct result of the spending pattern changes that occurred when computer systems did not crash when the date changed from 12/31/1999 to 1/1/2000. It was commonly and affectionately referred to as the Y2K problem. This business owner thought about closing his company. He thought long and hard about what he wanted from life and from his business. He talked with his wife, partner, children and employees about what was important. He got very clear on his intelligent self-interest.

Knowing this gentleman personally, I knew two things about him: his integrity was above reproach and when he gave his word it was his bond. As he thought through what he wanted, he came to this conclusion: "he wanted to be a business owner and he wanted to deliver what he told his customers he would deliver." He was very selfish in understanding what was important to him, and he made this clear to the important people in his life and engaged their support. The only people who got his attention during this time were people who wanted to buy his products and those who expressed interest in investing in his company.

He risked everything to accomplish his intelligent self-interest of being a business owner and delivering on his promises to his customers. He learned new skills. He created new relationships. For two years, the only food he and his family ate was food they could purchase with a coupon. His children did not get what they wanted for Christmas. His employees worked overtime without pay. It was hard. He was selfish with his time, money, and resources. Though it took effort, the company is now a thriving, successful organization. This achievement was the result of a business owner who got clear on his intelligent self-interest and the intelligent self-interest of his company, then took inspired action to achieve his greatness. This company will never be a Fortune 1000 company. The owner plans to sell when it reaches $10M in revenue. That's ok because this man is a success and there are thousands like him around the country and around the world.

This is the good kind of intelligent self-interest. By being selfish, he created a company that solved a need in the marketplace, he created a successful business that provided good jobs to his employees, and he created the type of life he wanted for his highest good and that of his family. He helped his employees by paying a good wage for good work. His selfishness paid handsomely for everyone involved. His selfishness led to action that allowed him to create his success. His selfishness was centered on being a successful business owner and doing what he told his customers he would do. He defined doing what he said he would do as integrity, and integrity is a core value for him in both his personal life and his business life.

Your intelligent self-interest must be a core value for you. This concept of creating and living by a core value has been lost in today's society. We are too concerned about political correctness and not offending others. We are overwhelmed by the accelerated pace of change. Because things change so fast we worry about being wrong or doing the wrong things. If your intelligent self-interest is a core value for you, you cannot be wrong. Values are a personal choice on how we choose to live our lives.

Simply putting a stake in the ground and telling others what we believe in and what we stand for can make others afraid, angry or both. But we must do this if we are to implement our intelligent self-interest as an individual and do the GREAT THINGS (emphasis intended) each of us can achieve.

We oftentimes prevent others from using their talents (or creating new talents) to achieve great things because of our core values. We might tell them it is too risky, not the right time, they are too old/young, etc. The idea of accomplishing great things seems to have been taken over by people who cannot or do not want to expend the effort (energy) to do great things themselves but who want to tell others how to expend their energies.

To truly have an INTELLIGENT (not self-centered) self-interest to create greatness, you MUST focus on the development of your own abilities, talents and core values and put them to their highest and best use. The only measurement we must use is NEVER thinking that our highest and best use must be at another person's expense. The development of our own intelligent self-interest is simply to allow us to do great things when called upon and being able to do so.

Taking inspired action to achieve "great things" is essential. A "great thing" is defined as an achievement beyond your normal achievements FOR others who cannot (not won't), and the great thing must be an achievement that is win-win for everyone involved. One primary test for achieving great things through the use of our intelligent self-interest is one of honesty. An athlete can win a world class event, but if the thin difference between being best and second best is performance-enhancing drugs, the outcome is failure. In this case "winning" is NOT "intelligent" self-interest. It is just self-interest. The key is "intelligent."

In this philosophy, "intelligent" means understanding your talent, ability, focus, effort, and truth, and choosing to apply them in a way that is a win for all parties involved. Intelligent self-interest is not necessarily about more money, fame, or national recognition, though that could happen. Selfishness is about the grandmother who starts a nonprofit to help sexually abused children; it is about the sister who starts a foundation to help others deal with breast cancer; it is about the mother who wants to put drunk drivers away; it is about the business owner who makes a commitment to his customers and delivers on that commitment regardless of the cost, because it is the right thing to do. These actions can stand intense scrutiny and they can stand on their own merits.

The actions of financial speculators and some of our leaders can be defined as SELFISH but never "intelligent" in their self-interest. They are never in it for win-win. They are in it for the win-lose; they win you lose. You only have to look at the Great Depression of the 1930s, the technology bubble of the late 1990s, and the mortgage fiasco of 2007 for examples.

The idea of using "intelligent self-interest" as a business success tool demands that we think differently about our dreams, desires, and expectations of who we are and what we can become and accomplish. We must understand selfishness is something required for success and that it is ok to be selfish! This selfishness provides the desire, the drive, and the need to take action. It is the gas that starts and keeps the engine running and the wheels moving forward.

Being a success is about taking healthy, calculated risks by creative and intelligent people who are aspiring to achieve their intelligent self-interest and accomplish great things. Each person is entitled to experience both the pain and benefits of the decisions they make. I believe that we are designed, from the time we are born, to actively create, grow and achieve. Starting a business is just one aspect of personal and business growth.

If you are not a business owner, you too can express the same intelligent self-interest in your chosen profession by being the best mother or father you can be, the best pastor, health care professional, nurse or waitress you can be.

Build your intelligent self-interest on a vision of what you want to achieve. Invest your company, profession or hobby with clarity of purpose. Build your intelligent self-interest to last not only for your lifetime but the lifetimes of your children and their children.

Every successful organization I have worked with has been clear on their intelligent self-interest and they have used this information to make decisions about what was right for the organization. Create your company and your life to last with a strong foundation, the foundation of intelligent self-interest.

What's Next?

Finally, here is a review of the nine principles this book is about. Our intelligent self-interest and being selfish about our intelligent self-interest is the first behavior. Our intelligent self-interest drives the other eight tools: ownership, results, persistence, discipline, focus, people, ideas and action.

The first step in the process is to give yourself permission to be selfish about what's important to you. I want to share with you an email I received after a discussion with a prospect.

"In my 57 years on this planet, no one has ever asked me how I define and measured success, until you. Since you posed that question to me, I have pondered it and came to the realization that I never set any metrics to measure MY success. I always strove for an objective others quantified as success - my parents, my family, my employer, etc. Was I deluding myself all these years? I realized, after our discussion, that I was measuring MY success based upon the approval of others. To say that this epiphany unsettled me is an understatement. I spent 57 years without a plan of my own - wandering moment to moment, reacting to others and events.

"I decided to make a pit stop in the race called life to determine a destination of MY choosing, my intelligent self-interest, and map out the most direct course to get there."

You too can make the same decision.

Here is a story of a gentleman, Ron McDaniel, who implemented all nine actions. His intelligent self-interest was to lose a significant amount of weight; specifically he wanted to weigh 140 pounds or less. My comments are in parentheses as I define the application of a specific principle.

"I hope you will forgive this more personal email from me. I spent about a day just wondering if I should share the story, because it is very personal and I certainly do not want to seem like I am bragging.

"Last September I read a blog post that completely changed my life. (It was from Tim Ferris, author of The Four Hour Work Week.) It did not seem like a huge deal that day, but it would be because it was the right information at the right time.

"I will get to the message in a second, but you people that are marketers or doing marketing for your business, please do not just read this story but also reflect on how a simple blog post changed everything for me (inspired action). Instead of wondering if you should set up a blog or how often you should post, maybe you should be asking yourself, 'Can I write something that will inspire someone to be better (to take action)?'

"On Friday, Aug. 9th I officially weighed 139.5 lb.

"Why am I sharing this? Well, in September of last year I was 186 lb and I read a blog post that said - eat these same things every day and don't eat flour and other 'bad' carbs. Exercise if you can. Cheat sometimes, but not more than once a week. (He stayed focused on what was important and he got ideas that helped him move closer to his intelligent self-interest.)

"I read that message and thought - I can do that. (He took ownership of his desired outcome and he took action to achieve his ideal weight.)

"I decided the day I read it that I would weigh less than 140 lb. (It is all about owning his results.)

"I am just very happy about reaching my goal and thought you might like to know about it. I also hope someone out there will read this and sometime in the future will write to me and say 'Thanks for sharing, you changed my life.' (His understand of people and the need to make a difference prompted his actions.)

"I do have one last thing I would like to tie in that is more marketing oriented. The entire concept of Buzzoodle is built on doing a little bit every day. (Here is persistence.)

"Whether you are trying to improve buzz marketing, lose weight or quit smoking, they all take a change in habits (persistence) and a daily commitment. And it will only succeed if it is your decision to succeed." (He defined his intelligent self-interest.)

15

Here is what Bill discovered as he developed his intelligent self-interest (ISI). Bill realized that he had failed in developing his ISI in the past because of obstacles with his belief systems. Bill shared the obstacles he found in creating his ISI. When Bill created his selfishness and it did not work, he needed to look at why this had happened. The importance of getting clear on your ISI cannot be stressed enough. Bill's first few attempts failed miserably but he did not stop trying to figure out what went wrong. Below are some of the things he found.

1. Bill's ISI needed to be consistent with his personal values and beliefs. He created intelligent self-interest that was not consistent with his beliefs and values and he lost interest because he created an inherent conflict between what he wanted to accomplish and who he was. He needed to either change his beliefs or his ISI. For example, he decided he initially wanted to make millions in real estate. But no matter how much he studied he just was not interested.

2. What Bill realized was that his ISI was not his. His first attempt at real estate was because his father-in-law owned real estate and he felt he could be successful there as well. When was not successful and he realized he was not interested, he tried again. He realized that ISI is too important to let someone else define it. He wanted it to be what he wanted to accomplish! Bill found this to be most important.

3. Bill's next pass at ISI was important to him but he was not inspired. After many years as a Fortune 1000 consultant he felt this much experience was too important to ignore. The more Bill worked this angle the less inspired he was. His heart just was not in it anymore. Bill realized if he could not get excited about his intelligent self-interest, he would lose interest. Bill wanted to create his ISI which would allow him to be passionate. He created a hairy goal that was exciting and risky at the same time.

4. Bill knew his ISI needed to be risky. He needed to put something out there that would inspire others to help him. This was risky for Bill because he did not know how other would respond. Bill knew that if there is no risk involved there can no be sense of accomplishment. If he were not stretching himself and moving outside his comfort zone, nothing would happen. Bill realized that reason leads to conclusion but emotion leads to action. Bill knew he needed to challenge himself.

5. Bill knew that, as he got clear on his ISI, that his ISI was necessary to setting great goals. Once his ISI was his primary purpose, he

could set clear goals with measurable objectives. Bill understood that goals are derived from his intelligent self-interest. We can have many goals that lead to ISI and Bill realized his goals changed as he got deeper into his ISI.

6. As Bill worked through his ISI he got so excited about what he wanted to accomplish that he set his intelligent self-interest too high and he set too many ISIs. It is just not possible to focus on more than one ISI. Bill found the common ground in his different ISIs and combined them so there was just one ISI. This was important to Bill because he did not want to overextend himself mentally, emotionally or financially.

7. Using a personal vision and mission statement Bill was able to focus on what it looks like to accomplish his ISI. He could feel it, see it and experience it in his mind. This was an important realization to Bill because he did not know how he would do this but he was clear on how it would feel. He planted this feeling in his mind and body by seeing and feeling the end results.

8. Bill realized he had to change how he thought. He needed to create new skills and talk with people who had been there before him, and they could show him the way. This meant he would need to change the people he associated with if they did not support his ISI. He started reading books, listening to audio programs, and doing visualization techniques that brought his ISI closer. He created self talk and thoughts that supported his ISI. He knew he could not have his ISI in mind and keep thinking about how it would not happen. The website was critical to Bill's success: www.ilearningglobal.biz/ronf

9. Bill came to a powerful realization as he controlled his self talk and thoughts. When he controlled his thoughts, he started the process of changing his attitude. He decided what attitude he wanted and focused on those thoughts. Bill found that thoughts about his ISI created the need for action; actions formed his habits; habits built his character; and this character changed his destiny.

10. Bill started taking action with simple steps. He knew that if he were to achieve his ISI, action was not only required but essential. Bill created a plan that got him started. He did not overanalyze because he knew that if he thought too much about it, he would find reasons it would not work. He believed that the road would reveal itself as he took action.

11. Any time Bill worked on something new, he knew he had to be

17

persistent. He kept a clear picture of his ISI in mind, and kept moving forward. Bill understood that when you are learning new skills it may take some time to become proficient, so he was patient with himself and he persisted in applying his new skills.

12. From his business experience, Bill knew that what he measured was what got his attention. He started measuring his progress: how many books he read, lesson learned, how the new actions worked (or did not work). He changed his behavior to focus more on what worked and less on what did not.

So what did Bill decide as his ISI?

1. That he was tired of bad news and he would start a conference that asked business owners to tell others what they did right so others could benefit from this knowledge.

2. That he would write a book on success and have it published within five years.

3. He would start is own company and his company would focus on helping business owners confidently take inspired action that leads to successful results, however these business owners define them.

In the next chapter we will discuss how Bill applied the concept of ownership in moving forward to his ISI.

CHAPTER 2:

OWNERSHIP - IF YOU DO NOT OWN IT YOU CANNOT CHANGE IT

"Freeing yourself was one thing; claiming ownership of that freed self was another."

–Toni Morrison

19

Ownership is critical to success because it is so empowering. It can be frightening, but empowering. Before we move into ownership let's discuss why it can be so frightening. Imagine, if you would, your life is a mess, you filed bankruptcy, your significant other left you, and the dog ran away. I am asking you to look in the mirror and say, "I created this. If I created this I can change it!" Can you do this? If you could, how do you think you would feel: frightened, angry, frustrated, confused, lonely? Do you think after you felt all these different negative emotions you would feel relieved and then empowered?

How did Bill come to understand this concept of ownership? When Bill lost his job as a result of 9/11 and Y2K, he fell into a deep depression. He was in a hole and he did not have a way to support his family without uprooting his family. The more he thought about this the more depressed he became. After months of frustration, Bill sought the help of a counselor who understood his situation. After a few weeks, Bill came to understand that he was depressed because he felt helpless to do anything about the situation. Bill was used to taking charge and making things happen, and he felt he was in a situation in which he had no control.

After much soul searching, Bill knew that if he were to change his situation he had to take ownership for where he was. This was tough for Bill because he could not do anything about the economy. Experience taught him there were no jobs within 100 miles of his home. The economy shut down as a result of 9/11.

When Bill realized his depression was the result of a feeling he could not control his destiny, he decided he needed to do something. He talked with his wife and they decided he would relocate to anywhere he could get a job. Both he and his wife decided to let his daughter finish high school (she was a sophomore). He talked to his daughter and told her of the decision he had made. She offered to go to summer school and finish school a year early. He asked her why she would give up Latin Club, Character Counts and being Captain of the soccer team. She simply said she did not want to be away from him for two years. At that point in time Bill made two major decisions: his skills were good and there was no reason to be unemployed, and he would do something about the bad news being written about in the local newspaper.

There was no reason to leave his home and his family. Bill could start his business where he lived. Bill finally understood ownership. Now the real work of ownership started. Bill was very afraid and very excited. He got angry that he bought into belief systems that led him to helplessness. He was initially angry at his parents for enabling this victim mentally. Finally, Bill came to accept where he was. He realized that if he accepted the belief systems he had, he could change them. But first he had to own them and realize they were his. Once he came to this realization, he knew he could examine them and keep the beliefs he wanted and change the ones that no longer served him. After he accepted the situation he felt empowered to change things. This was the point where Bill decided he needed to act upon his ISI and start taking inspired action.

Now let's define ownership and discuss how ownership differs from responsibility.

Ownership is the legal right of possession. In the simplest terms, it empowers you to embrace your intelligent self-interest. Ownership says not only am I responsible for my life and where it is right now, but ownership goes one step farther. Ownership says I am allowed to pursue my dreams, my goals, and my highest ideals.

When you take ownership of your situation, it allows you to make changes and do things differently. Ownership empowers you to act, to take action. As you will see in the chapter on success, ownership is a critical component. Let's see how one person handled this issue of ownership.

"My name is Maureen Gechter and I am a probate and bankruptcy attorney. One of the most significant things I have learned is a different way of thinking. I have moved my thinking to one of ownership and empowerment. Instead of thinking of a problem or a person as too difficult to deal with, my thinking has changed to one of why give my power over to such a problem/person. It puts the problem/person in perspective and gives me the ability to resolve the problem/person without the stress that I normally feel. The most surprising aspect was finding that the principles (in this book) have affected not only my professional life, but also my private life. Through ownership I am exploring opportunities that I never felt I could explore in the past and I am seeing things in an entirely different way. If I created the situation, I can change the situation."

21

Ownership is different from responsibility and more powerful. Responsibility is defined in Webster's Dictionary as "on one's own initiative or authority." Ownership is a "legal right of possession." I do not know about you but I want the legal right to my intelligent self-interest. I then can take initiative (responsibility) to make things happen.

When you take responsibility you are implying that there is someone else who has actual ownership of your situation. In business that is not uncommon. Your boss has ownership for getting something done and he may delegate to you and give you responsibility for making it happen. Your boss has ownership for the success or failure of a given project. He may hold you accountable but the management team is asking him the hard questions. If your boss decides to do the work himself he has both ownership and responsibility for the project.

What are the outcomes of ownership? When you take ownership of something you have empowered yourself, taken the responsibility to make change. If you do not own it you cannot change it. If you do not own your intelligent self-interest, you cannot achieve it. The outcome of ownership is peace of mind. Your problems don't go away but you will sleep better because you are taking action to achieve your intelligent self-interest.

What are the attributes of being an owner? You set goals that allow you to move forward toward your intelligent self-interest. You define the results needed for success, put a process in place to measure those results, find out what works, implement the discipline to allow others to achieve the same results, and understand who needs to be involved as well as the skills required. You are focused on the desired outcome by measuring the results. You are persistent in trying new things. You search for ideas to take you closer to your ISI.

Tell yourself right now that you own your current situation. You may not know why you are in this situation, but once you take ownership of where you are, you are now empowered to change it. Ownership is learning to think differently. Own your thinking process, own your results, own your life and know you can change the outcome from here forward because you are empowered to take inspired action to achieve your desired results and your intelligent self-interest.

A true story might help you better understand this concept.

In one of my Business Mastery Advisory Boards (www.rpfgroupinc.com), a member, through some bad decisions, lost control of his company. He was a mess and he second-guessed everything he had ever done and questioned everything he was wanting to achieve. As a result of his past decisions, he joined the Business Mastery Advisory Board to gain clarity on what had happened and to avoid the same situation moving forward. For the longest time he blamed his partner, their lawyer, everyone but himself for this situation. Once the members of his Advisory Board helped him understand that he was the only one who could make the decisions, he accepted ownership, then responsibility, for his actions. After all, he signed the documents. He listened to his advisors. He selected his advisors. Once he realized it was his decision, and he owned the decision making process and the outcome of his decision, he was empowered to move past it and start another company. This time he used his Advisory Board to help structure his decision making process in a manner that protected him.

From ownership, Bill was able to formulate a series of goals and he determined the results he wanted to achieve. In the next chapter we will discuss results. Results are the strong outcome of ownership. Results help you determine the correct course of action.

CHAPTER 3:

IT IS NOT ABOUT ACCOMPLISHMENTS - IT IS ABOUT RESULTS

"Results! Why, man, I have gotten a lot of results. I know several thousand things that won't work."

–Thomas A. Edison

25

In our prior chapters we talked about the importance of intelligent self-interest or selfishness and taking ownership. Now we will turn our attention to results, or more correctly, measuring everything.

Busyness does not count. Efficiency does not count. Only effectiveness counts. For our purposes I define effectiveness as any action that takes us toward the accomplishment of our intelligent self-interest.

You are probably asking yourself, "What is the difference between efficiency and effectiveness?"

Since you asked, let me explain.

Efficiency is doing things right.

Effectiveness is doing the right things.

The first goal Bill set was to start a business conference to showcase successful businesses so he could learn from them and help them grow through great exposure. He began sharing his idea with others and over time he built a team of six people who liked his vision and agreed to help. The first order of business was to create an event that others would contribute both time and money to. Bill talked about how much money he needed and how to raise it, and assigned people to solicit sponsorships. He created attendance goals. He created judging criteria to determine what a successful company looked like. The team created a nomination form and marketing material to get the word out.

The first conference required Bill to interview all 41 business owner to see what they did. From this interview process a story was written and used by the judges. An interesting thing happened: Bill created his first book.

Bill learned what others did to be successful and he decided to begin implementing the behaviors he was learning about. One of the conference founders, Don Philabaum, had this to say as Bill shared his idea of measuring everything.

> "You are taught when you are young to share, not yell, be co-operative and get along with others. However, as you grow older you begin to run into a wider circle of people who are coming from all different walks of life, all different behavior

styles and very different moral centers. When you are given an opportunity to run your department or even a business, the number one thing you need to keep in mind is RESULTS. You need to understand, as a business owner, your place is not to be nice but to get things done.

The best way to lead your group is to set process benchmarks, establish what will happen when process benchmarks are not reached and then enforce them. Part of process benchmarks is a clear definition of the roles and responsibilities of all process participants. The entire company depends on each person within the company delivering their agreed upon results in order for the organization to function smoothly. Without clearly defined processes, roles and responsibilities it is almost impossible to take swift action because no goals have been set. When goals (benchmarks) are defined it is easier to take swift action when the results are not reached. There are usually two reasons results are not achieved: Either the system is broken or someone in the system is failing.

From years of experience, my recommendation is to retrain and reaffirm with the individuals who are not reaching their goals and let them go if they do not improve. Many times this is a hard decision, but if you fail to make it, your entire company will suffer. A colleague of mine once said to me, "Your company is only as strong as the weakest employee." Remember that and do whatever it takes to manage your department and company for RESULTS driven by your company's intelligent self-interest."

Bill realized that if he did not measure everything, how would he know he was being effective?

A client's company was very efficient at all the wrong things because they measured how quickly they did things internally but the things they measured did not reflect the needs of the customer or the needs of the market. The actions they needed to be effective at were not being measured at all. Consequently, they were very efficient but not at all effective. This internal focus resulted in a competitor entering

27

the market who could deliver a product at a lower cost than my client could build it.

One of the things the owner realized was that he had the wrong definition of what success meant to him. His intelligent self-interest needed clarity. He bought into the belief that success was having a big company with lots of employees. This was a problem because he did not want to manage people. He did not have the time or the interest and this was a source of stress for him. It took him away from what was important to him, his selfishness.

He wanted to create and sell new products. As the trust grew in our relationship, I was able to help him understand what was in his best intelligent self-interest. After he got clear, he sold his company and started a new company writing books and consulting on his passion, creating Internet strategies for companies. His new business model is very different; no employees and each project must meet his requirements for one-page partnerships, as he calls them. He is happier and more effective than he has ever been.

When you perform your daily activities but you are not clear on what you want to accomplish (your intelligent self-interest), how do you know you are doing the right things? Remember, right things means being effective, moving toward your intelligent self-interest, not being efficient at things that keep you busy but don't move you forward to your intelligent self-interest.

A client, who is great at networking, did not get any business for her efforts. Her understanding of networking was meeting with everyone who wanted to meet with her. Since she is an accountant by trade, she had no problems getting people to meet with her. Almost without exception each meeting ended with a request for her to open up her customer base to do joint marketing. Rarely was there a good reason for her to do this.

After she hired me, I asked her why she was meeting with a specific person. She answered, "Isn't that what networking is all about?"

I then asked her what outcome she wanted.

"I do not know."

"Let me ask you again. Why are you meeting with him?"

"I do not know."

"If you are meeting people (networking) without a clear objective of what you want from each meeting, how effective can you be?"

"Not very."

I said, "If you are meeting 20 people a week, you are certainly efficient are creating networking opportunities, but how effective are you in moving towards your goal?"

Since we talked about ownership, she felt empowered to create an effective networking strategy.

I asked her the following questions as she was creating her strategy:

- "What do you want to accomplish from each meeting?"

- "Who is the best person for you to meet with to achieve your intelligent self-interest?"

- "Is a next step always defined? If not, why not?"

- "What is the investment in terms of time, energy and money of creating this relationship, and is it worth it?"

- "Is the return on investment clearly measured for time, energy and money?"

When she started getting clear on what she wanted from her networking, her business grew 40% in less than a year. She moved from being very efficient at networking to being very effective at networking.

Another client figured out that each networking event he missed cost him $88. He knew where his business came from and it came from networking. So he scheduled his time most effectively by attending more networking events. He attends four networking events weekly.

Before we move too much farther, let's take a minute to define results.

Results, as defined by *Webster's Dictionary*, are a "consequence of a specific action." Since you are taking ownership of your life, your intelligent self-interest, start measuring everything. Find out what works. Determine the consequences of your actions. Measuring results allows you to spend your time effectively on achieving your selfishness, your intelligent self-interest.

Just a reminder; before you can measure results you must take ownership for the outcomes you are experiencing in your life. Once you take ownership, you can start measuring your results, your effectiveness. Once you define what works, you can create discipline in your life.

When Bill was successful at defining what worked, he realized he needed to implement a discipline that allowed others to do the same things. The successful business owners he interviewed call this discipline. Discipline allows you to take what works and make it a measurable, repeatable, and predictable process that leads to both personal and corporate habits. Speaking of discipline...

CHAPTER 4:

DISCIPLINE IS CREATING MEASURABLE, REPEATABLE, AND PREDICTABLE SUCCESS HABITS

"Age acquires no value save through thought and discipline."

–James Truslow Adams

In prior chapters we talked about the importance of intelligent self-interest or selfishness, measuring results, and taking ownership.

Let's turn our attention to discipline and spend some time understanding what discipline is and how to implement it. When I talk about discipline, I am not talking about the discipline someone else imposes on us. No one likes being forced to do things they do not like. I am talking about a different kind of discipline: the creation of measurable, repeatable, and predictable actions that lead to measurable, predictable, repeatable results.

Many of us suffer because we have bad habits that we created (remember ownership). Those habits worked for us at the time. When we realized they worked, we used them over and over again. We created a habit. That is all a habit is, a measurable, repeatable, predictable process or action.

How did Bill apply this concept? When he realized how to raise sponsorship money for the conference, he created a process and trained other how to do this. This freed him to work on the next process: getting the word out. After the first conference, word got out via work of mouth. Each of the members spoke to different organization and emailed their people on their email lists. This worked well the first year because they had 20 speakers and over 200 attendees. Now Bill needed to figure a way to get the word out that was not so time intensive.

Bill took what he learned in acquiring sponsors and went after companies (business magazines and chambers of commerce) that would benefit from being involved in this event. Two major companies stepped up to help market the event.

How does this concept apply in your business? If I am in sales, I may know that to close one sale, I need to make 50 calls. When I make my 50 calls, I get 10 appointments. From the 10 appointments, I make one sale. This is a measurable, repeatable and predictable process. I know that if I make 50 calls and do not get 10 appointments, then I need to change my approach to getting appointments. If I am getting my 10 appointments but not making my one sale, I know I need to change how I close.

Once I figure out how to make my 50 calls, get my 10 appointments and make one sale, I do the same thing over and over and over again. What I've done is to create a habit: measure, repeatable and predictable. As a business owner you can now train all new sales representatives on this process. The new sales representative can now achieve the same predictable results.

How would this work in a personal relationship? If I am in a relationship with someone and we are always fighting (fighting is my results), I can define the outcome I want (intelligent self-interest). I can measure the change in the relationship by the reduction in the number of fights. Since I am taking ownership of the situation, I am empowered to change how I respond to the individual. Since I chose to respond differently, I can expect different results. Didn't I just create a measurable, repeatable and predictable process?

When I get the results I want, I can choose to implement those actions regularly.

Let's get more specific for those of you who want more but do not want to be bored to tears by books that explain this in detail. We will talk about business first.

Every company has processes; some are clearly defined, others are implicit. Business processes are the way a business does things. Many companies I've worked with talk about the need to continuously improve their business processes to reduce cost, and become more efficient, effective and productive.

The need to redesign a business process can occur for several reasons: mergers or acquisitions, inefficiencies, cost control, lack of process effectiveness, competition and global pressures, just to name a few.

Characteristics that would indicate a business process is a candidate for improvement include any process that has inherent delays, transportation and storage requirements, low ownership and accountability, high rework, significant paper handling, reappearance of the same problems, high waste, a poor feedback system, focus on quantity not quality, long cycle times, and long process times.

As important as it is to continuously improve your business processes,

33

be careful not to become so internally focused that your relationships with your clients suffer. Many companies see great results in designing or redesigning processes and over time they spend more time working on the activities of the process instead of focusing on the expected or intended outcomes of improving the process.

One company I worked for refused to let a proposal go out the door until it was reviewed by more than 20 people during a monthly two-day configuration review meeting. This resulted in the sales organization finding ways to circumvent the process in order to be more responsive to clients. In many cases the configurations being reviewed were not the same configurations being presented to the clients. The process just took too long.

How do you approach business process improvement? The methodology described below is one I use for all my business process improvement projects. Here is what Bill learned as he created measurable, repeatable and predictable processes for his business and the conference. Don't be frightened by this; it is short and sweet.

1. **Planning & Organization** - Know what you want the redesign to accomplish: drive out cost, make the company more responsive, implement an empowering employee culture, etc. Know who the process owner is. There is ownership and intelligent self-interest in this step.

2. **Data Gathering & Recording** - What data do you need to gather? How do you gather that information? How does the data gathered support the project objectives? Is the right data being gathered? There we go measuring again.

3. **Analyze Data** - Take what you learn and create a baseline process. After the baseline is complete you can better understand the implications of making a change to the existing process. Here we find out what works.

4. **Redesign the process** - Redesign the process to drive the expected actions, cost savings, or productivity defined in the planning and organization phase of the project. Make sure the new process is consistent with the objective of the redesign. This is where discipline begins: the creation of a measurable, repeatable, and predictable process.

5. **Analyze Risks** - Understand the risks associated with the planned

changed. Do a risk analysis and create a contingency plan in the event certain risks materialize. Here we are redesigning the process because we are not happy with the results we were getting. Here we analyze those risks to ensure we do not propagate the same errors into the new process.

6. **Create Implementation Plan** - Many times when processes are changed, companies fail to integrate the new process and tools into the business. It becomes an add-on that just creates more work without reaching the desired results. The implementation plan is designed to drive effectiveness not efficiency. When we focus on effectiveness we will implement the correct amount of efficiency.

7. **Create Cost Benefits Analysis** - There is a review of expected cost and benefits during each step of the process. This step is nothing more than the formalization of what you have learned in the prior steps. We are back to effectiveness here.

8. **Implement your plan.** This is the action step.

Notice that all nine actions are inherent in these eight steps.

Many of the processes Bill initially created failed. What Bill realized was that he needed to design the process to drive the behavior that he wanted his volunteers to implement. This is important because systems drive processes; processes drive behaviors; behaviors drive results. **When you want to change the results you must change the behavior.** So once Bill understood what behaviors were necessary to raise money, he create a process to allow anyone to raise money.

Here is how one person used this concept to change his business and get more personal time.

"As a multiple-business owner, there are times when you have to consider where your time can be best spent. The NewTide Group is a small Internet marketing and web design firm. I was doing fairly well.

However, it was a very time consuming proposition, as I was personally involved in the project management of nearly every client's website development and marketing. Opportunities for residual income in my other business

35

opportunities were becoming more appealing, but the time required to operate NewTide was inhibiting my ability to take advantage of them. In the interest of future success, I was considering selling NewTide in order to consolidate my efforts.

I don't have to be holding the reigns constantly anymore.

Here's what I did. The solution seems so simple now...

NewTide's business works off of an independent contractor and partner model. Through key relationships with 3rd party companies and independent professionals, we're able to assemble the teams necessary to produce effective results at competitive prices. The problem was, I always ended up being the "hub" for the contractors. If we were "building a house" I was the General Contractor.

Over time, I had developed especially valuable relationships with exceptional individuals and companies. I relied on them for their ability to perform the technical work, but I had never empowered them to step up and work as project managers, dealing directly with clientele to solve problems. It occurred to me, some of these individuals already had the skill set necessary to do this... they were either already doing it with other customers of their own or, by working with me over the years, they were performing many of the same communication and problem solving skills necessary anyway!

One project at a time, I took the leap of faith and put these key people in the position of project manager. They were responsible for regular communication with clientele and the putting out of fires that previously I had to address. My communications are now largely consolidated into a few key people, rather than the entire company: every customer, every time.

They key point here is, these are independent contractors

(I.C.), not employees. Some people might think that placing this much customer relationship power in the hands of an I.C. is suicide. I feel that, in this day and age, employees and I.C.s aren't much different in that respect.... Employees can have even less loyalty to your company than your contractors can, because they're not building a business reputation the same way an I.C. is. The keys are: Long term relationships; Trust; and yes, compensation. I pay my people well... they get bonuses for work done beyond expectations. I pay them for work that goes beyond scope, even if I have to take the costs off of my profits.

Our next step is to take this same model into the sales arena, developing independent technical sales reps that work off of leads that our company's marketing provides. Again, there are key individuals who show potential for this kind of work; let's give them the opportunity to explore it, and everyone can benefit.

Build trust, loyalty, and respect with everyone, and you can build an empire.

Something I should add: **A big part of what makes this work is systems. Having procedural expectations in place, so there can be replicable processes and results. It's what helps ensure consistency, and keeps you as the owner in the loop with much more efficient communication."**

Jason Dutt

Notice how Jason created measurable, repeatable, predictable processes that drove the behaviors that helped make his company a success. This impacted not only NewTide but allowed him to capitalize on other business opportunities.

These same concepts work in your personal life as well. Let's discuss how this might work. Remember Ron McDaniel and how he lost weight; he ate the same healthy foods, exercised at the same time every day, and surrounded himself with people who supported his weight loss goal. These concepts work in business and your personal life.

Bill realized that people were critical to the success of the conference, so he started seeking ways to become more effective in his relationship with others.

In the next chapter we will discuss people. Your success and my success are 100% dependent on our ability to communicate, inspire, lead, motivate, coach, influence and sell ourselves and our ideas to others. Here comes the people side of the nine actions. You were waiting for this one, weren't you?

CHAPTER 5:

INSPIRING OTHERS TO SUCCESSFUL ACTION

"Our success is very much dependent on how effective we are at influencing, persuading, motivating, leading, educating and selling others to take inspired action."

–Ron Finklestein

In our prior chapters we talked about the importance of intelligent self-interest or selfishness, measuring results, taking ownership, and applying discipline to create measurable, repeatable, predictable habits. Now we turn our attention to The Platinum Rule® "treating others the way they want to be treated."

The Platinum Rule is used with the permission of Dr. Tony Alessandra.

Before we talk about *The Platinum Rule*, let's hear from a new business owner and how his people skills helped him be successful from Day One. He defined success as being profitable the day he started his business.

"People who want to Help People

I am a small business owner of less than a year. During my first year, unlike most small businesses, I have not struggled to find prospective customers nor to generate sales.

How have I managed to accomplish this? What is my secret? Are you sitting down? Take a deep breath. I am about to take a sledgehammer to all you've learned from the school of traditional small business development.

I have not been successful in generating leads and closing sales because I had a grand written business plan (though I do have a plan). It is not because of a great sales team; I am my sales team. It is not because I had the perfect logo, marketing materials, and advertisements that I placed in all the right places; I designed everything myself and until this past month I had spent less than $1,000 on advertising, most of which was spent on copies of flyers. Last, I have not been successful because I had a state-of-the-art website that was drawing hundreds of thousands of site visits per day. A guy from my church designed my website, and to date I have had less than 1,000 website visitors, most of which were probably me just checking my website to make sure it is still alive!

(*Note: All of the above mentioned items do play their necessary role in developing a business and are all things

I am currently addressing as a means to further grow my business.)

So, how did I do it? It is simple. People! Through genius, or more likely through pure luck, I have realized an important and fundamental truth: People want to help people.

During the first few months of my business, I attended an average of five networking events per week (COSE, International Referral Network (IRN), Trade Shows, Business Expos, and local Chambers of Commerce). I still attend at least three networking events per week, and I am a member of both COSE and the Medina IRN chapter. I attend these events and engage myself in as many conversations as I can. I always make a point to first learn about them and their business and how I might be able to help them, and then, I introduce my business and show them how they can assist me. When asked to assist, especially after I have already shown a genuine interest in him or her and what they do, people want to help me. People want to refer business to me. I have created a free sales team by simply meeting people, then showing and allowing them to help me.

Caution! This will only work when you approach people with a genuine interest in him or her and what they do; when you have a persistent follow-up plan; when you take action on your follow-up plan; and when you apply the needed discipline to carry out those actions.

I am a small business owner, and my sales our driven by people who want to help people."

Kevin Kelly
Convenient Car Cleaning
www.convenient-car-cleaning.com

Bill had a problem. As the conference grew, more people wanted to be involved and all were volunteers. He needed a way to quickly understand a person's strength, if they could do what they said they would do, and most importantly he needed to understand how to motivate his team. Since this was new to him, he embraced The Platinum Rule with enthusiasm. Here is what Bill learned as run ran the conference.

1. Don't try to change people.

2. Focus on having others do what they are good at.

3. Developing people does not mean getting them ready to move up in the organization but it does mean helping them find the best fit within the organization.

4. Development is helping others develop skills that help them build on what is important to them as it pertains to organizational success.

5. People do not want to be sold but they do want to be taught how to buy.

Bill used *The Platinum Rule*[1] to help with all five goals.

Being good with people is about getting them focused on their strengths and helping them build on what they already do well. It is taking ownership for providing opportunities for development, it is being persistent in making opportunities happen, it is teaching people why specific actions are important, and it is identifying and creating win/win situations in implementing your intelligent self-interest.

I want to tell you a story about what can happen if you do not understand people, your role in the relationship, and how people want to be treated. A business associate received this email from a hoped-to-be client. He was quite surprised and rightfully so.

Dear Joe (not his real name),

We decided we will not be getting insurance through you. I was quite disturbed at what happened at the Trade Show. You put my wife on the spot where she had to choose between embarrassing you or making you feel uncomfortable by not responding to your comment. My wife always does her utmost not to cause discomfort for anyone. It would have been one thing if you were not aware. I think we have shown you kindness. We have welcomed your questions about ourselves, even at a great inconvenience to us and even though the conversation was a bit intrusive. We did that as a kindness. But for us, I prefer to do business with someone who first shows us respect and who can understand our needs.

Signed,
Not happy with the relationship

What could he have done differently?

We can observe the behavior of people we are with and treat them how *they* want to be treated and not how *we* want to be treated.

When we treat others the way we want to be treated, we can experience all kinds of relationship problems. I use *The Platinum Rule* for better understanding people and how to treat them the way them want to be treated.

The Platinum Rule is a safe, easy to understand, and effective tool to increase personal productivity, reduce stress in relationships, and create better effectiveness. What many people do not understand is that success and personal effectiveness go hand in hand. **Our success is very much dependent on how effective we are at influencing, persuading, motivating, leading, educating and selling others to take inspired action. The Platinum Rule will show us how to do this.**

People want to know that we trust them. Most of the time, when people buy into our vision and feel they can contribute, they will be loyal and productive. For trust to develop, especially in an organization, roles and responsibilities must be clearly defined. Many

43

people thrive on knowing what they are allowed to do and what they are not allowed to do. When you put people in a position to succeed, the result can be powerful. That is what *The Platinum Rule* is all about: putting people in a position to succeed.

What happens when people are successful? Production increases, morale improves, and people want to stay in your organization or be around you because they know you will trust them to do the right thing. *The Platinum Rule* is about creating that type of relationship. Because there is so much written on The Platinum Rule, I will not go into significant detail. The information we are discussing in this chapter, for those of you who want more details, can be found in *The Platinum Rule for Small Business Mastery*, available on Amazon.com.

We all know people are different. Yet many of us have never been taught how to build effective relationships. Since we are all members of the human race, it is expected that we would develop those skills from our teachers, parents and role models. That's fine if your role model, parent, or teachers are experts in identifying and creating these relationships. Most of us have never had those kinds of coaches, mentors, role models or teachers.

Because we did not have experts to teach us, we need to take ownership ourselves for learning this skill. That is where The *Platinum Rule* comes into play.

Though *The Platinum Rule* is easy to learn, it requires practice to become proficient, like any new skill. That is why persistence is so important.

Charles Darwin made this comment. "It is not the strongest of species that survive, nor the most intelligent, but the one most responsive to change." *The Platinum Rule* will teach you adaptability strategies that will allow you to be more responsive to change. When you read the section below, you will learn how to build trust faster, create better relationship more easily, and take the stress out of your relationships. How do I know? I've already done all that by using The *Platinum Rule*.

When I teamed up with Dr. Tony Alessandra and Scott Zimmerman to write *The Platinum Rule® for Small Business Mastery*, I wanted to communicate that your success and my success are very much dependent on how well we communicate, influence, motivate, lead, counsel, sell and

"The Platinum Rule® is a registered trademark of Dr. Tony Alessandra. Used with permission.

persuade those we deal with on a daily basis. *The Platinum Rule for Small Business Mastery* takes 12 areas of business and discusses how to apply *The Platinum Rule*® for more and faster success.

As I work with people who experience success, I have realized that these individuals are the ones who seem to understand the importance of others and the role they play in making success possible. The others I am referring to are the employees who work for us, customers who buy from us, the families who inspire and depend on us for their physical, emotional and psychological needs, and the friends who enjoy our company.

A few years ago, I was teaching a class on *The Platinum Rule*. At the end of the class, one of the participants (a director in a Fortune 100 company) came up to me and asked, "Why didn't they teach me this in high school?" I could not answer that question then, but I think I know the answer now. I think, because we are a part of the human race, people expect us to acquire this skill from our parents, and from interaction with our peers and from others we deal with regularly. I am not sure that is a valid assumption, especially if the people teaching us have not acquired the necessary skills.

The Platinum Rule® will allow you to: lower interpersonal tension and increase trust, know your own behavioral tendencies, recognize the behavioral style of others, and adapt your style for success.

I asked Dr. Tony Alessandra to provide an overview of how you might treat others the way they want to be treated. Here is what he had to say:

> "Has the Golden Rule lost its glitter? Absolutely not! The Golden Rule has as much "glitter" as ever. I believe and practice it 110%, especially when it comes to values, ethics, honesty and consideration. However, when it comes to interpersonal communication, it can very well backfire. The Golden Rule states, "Do unto others as you would have them do unto you." Basically translated, that says to treat others the way you would like to be treated, which of course isn't always the case.

> An addition to the Golden Rule is The *Platinum Rule*: "Treat

45

others the way they want to be treated." The focus of the relationship shifts from "this is what I want, so I'll give every-one the same thing" to "let me first understand what they want, and then I'll give it to them."

The goal of *The Platinum Rule* is personal chemistry and productive relationships. You don't have to change your personality. You simply have to understand what drives people and recognize your options for dealing with them. *The Platinum Rule* divides behavioral preferences into four behavioral styles: Director, Socializer, Relater, and Thinker. Everyone possesses the qualities of each style to various degrees and everyone has a dominant style. The key to us-ing The Platinum Rule is to understand a person's domi-nant personality style and treat him/her appropriately.

Here is a very basic breakdown of the behavior styles de-fined by The *Platinum Rule*:

Directors are driven by two governing needs: to control and achieve. They are goal-oriented go-getters who are most comfortable when they are in charge of people and situa-tions.

Socializers are friendly, enthusiastic and like to be where the action is. They thrive on admiration, acknowledgment, and compliments. They are idea people who excel at getting others excited about their vision.

Thinkers are analytical, persistent, systematic people who enjoy problem solving. They are detail-oriented, which makes them more concerned with content than style. Thinkers are task-oriented people who enjoy perfecting processes and working toward tangible results.

Relaters are warm and nurturing individuals. They are the most people-oriented of the four styles. Relaters are excellent listeners, devoted friends, and loyal employees. They are good planners, persistent workers, and good with follow-through."

The Platinum Rule provides powerful life skills that will serve you well in all your relationships: business, friends, family, spouse, and children.

I want to discuss learning and applying *The Platinum Rule* and why *The Platinum Rule* is so important. More and more businesses derive their value from the intellectual capital of the people in the organization: accountants, consultants, engineers, information technology, architects, financial advisors, sales professionals, and the list goes on. When someone leaves an organization, that intellectual capital leaves with them. Where does it usually go? To a competitor! They now know your marketing and sales strategy, your company's value proposition, and all the problems in your company. Do you think that puts your organization in a tough situation? I do, and it also gives your competitor some very clear ways to compete with and beat you.

This means relationships are key: relationships with employees, customers, suppliers, and partners. You must be good at building effective relationships. Genuinely caring about others is the most effective, as well as the most satisfying, way to do this.

I teach *The Platinum Rule* from two perspectives: dealing with difficult people and creating better relationships. Dealing with difficult people discusses how to identify and respond to difficult people. When I teach this material, I spend a lot of time on personal beliefs. Many times I find the attendees expect others to know what they are thinking. Early on in the class I tell people I am not a mind reader. So I ask many questions to get clarity when necessary. When I teach creating better relationships, I focus on what works and how to do more of the same.

In my class I tell this story about my wife (with her permission of course!). One time she was upset about something that happened at work. I assumed she was asking for some help (advice). I made what I thought were some good suggestions. She stopped right in the middle of our discussion and said, "All I want you to do is listen." I realized I was treating her how I would want to be treated in that situation. That was an incorrect assumption. For the longest time, when we talked, I would ask my wife what she wanted. "Do you want me to listen or do you want help?" This eliminates many disagreements in our house. Now, my wife starts the discussion with, "Can you just listen?" or "Would you help me?" Either way I know what is expected of me and this allows me to treat my wife the way she wants to be treated.

47

When I tell this story in my workshops, many of the ladies get upset with me. They assume I should know what to do without asking. The gentlemen in my class really like the idea of asking that question. I tell everyone that I am not a mind reader and without questions I cannot understand the situation. I ask for their patience and by the time the workshop is over they better understand the value of the question.

One of the things I find in these classes is that people are afraid to ask questions. We are taught not to pry or ask why. We don't want to look stupid. As a child, how many times did you hear "Because I said so?" I was taught as a child not to ask for anything because the answer would be no. This was both a blessing and a curse. A blessing because I learned to be self-sufficient; a curse because it would have been so much easier if I had told people what I wanted instead of assuming "no" would be the answer. It took me years to understand that people appreciate being asked questions, provided they are asked in the correct manner. The correct manner is using *The Platinum Rule* and understanding the person's specific behavior style. I then ask my questions in a manner they will find most pleasing to receive and understand.

So How Do You Use This Information?

Here is a story about how one person learned how to find people who would help him be successful.

> "I'm sure everyone reading this has heard the statement, "It's not what you know BUT who you know." Most of us accept the statement to be true to some degree. This doesn't mean what you know is not important because in today's world who you know doesn't mean much if you can't do the job. But since time began who you know has played a critical role in success. I entered the staffing industry 28 years ago and it seems every year since I have attended conferences, read books, viewed videos and attended webinars on the subject of how to meet more people that can help my business. The challenge has always been meeting the right people and knowing how to utilize that relationship.
>
> For years I thought meeting the right people meant being

well connected. I joined local and national organizations, and became active as an officer in several giving it 120% effort. The results were rewarding but generally had little impact on my business results and certainly didn't justify the time and money I invested.

I began to realize that meeting the right people for me was like trying to hit a moving target because each staffing assignment had unique skills with unique requirements even though I have always specialized in Information Technology. I knew there had to be a solution that allowed me to focus on key people in organizations and maximize my relationship value in a minimum of time. From a business perspective the concept of "MRV" Maximum Relationship Value is the key to achieving goals and sustaining success. This Value only exists if you are receiving more benefits from the time invested than you would using that same amount of time on any other function.

Gaining MRV was made more difficult because to achieve sustained success required developing mutual benefit (treating others the way they want to be treated).

Therefore, I not only had to identify the right person but I also had to identify what would benefit them. This meant I had to know a lot more about them than where they worked and what they did. This involved a lot of research but the benefits were improving and I was encouraged by the results. However the time investment was significant and I wasn't satisfied I was really achieving my goal of MRV.

Then two things happened that made achieving MRV not only possible but created an empowering environment where MRV became the natural result.

I was introduced to LinkedIn by a colleague who was attending a conference I was hosting. He made the comment that there was a new online network that allowed you to become directly involved with thousands of people.

49

Naturally I was interested but skeptical so I went online and checked it out. At first glance it didn't seem like much but I did some research and started talking to people that were successfully using this tool and gained an appreciation for what LinkedIn could do. Today I have over 2100 direct contacts and over 11,000,000 professionals in my LinkedIn network. I can go online to find an individual with the specific skills I am looking for, review their background, find out what is important to them, who they work with now, who they have worked with in the past and a bounty of information about their company and competitors. I can do all this before I ever send an email or make a phone call. I was now able to focus in on specific companies and individuals but I really didn't understand networking and how to maximize these relationships.

Most people are not natural networkers and at best achieve superficial results from their efforts. I started to understand networking when I attended a Chamber of Commerce dinner where the president of the organization was being honored for the work he had done in the community. I had the pleasure of sitting next to him at the dinner and naturally a conversation ensued about his work with the Chamber and what he did for a living. His name was Dan Minick and he said he was the president and CEO of a networking organization. This intrigued me because I didn't feel my results from networking had been that effective and now I was sitting beside someone who was the president of a national networking organization. I asked Dan what service he felt his organization provided and his answer made the hairs on my neck stand up. He said, "My organization is the International Referral Network, IRN, and we teach our members the concepts, principles and activities necessary to become proficient business networkers." One simple statement and it offered up the solution to my being able to achieve Maximum Relationship Value. Dan told me how members learned to present their companies to others effectively in 30 seconds, how they learned to gain maximum exposure and results from any business or social gathering and increase their business through direct referrals and many other benefits. I was hooked and after doing my research joined IRN.

The combination of utilizing LinkedIn to find key individuals and IRN to maximize my relationships and constantly gain new techniques to identify my services for others was a winner and allowed me to gain MAXIMUM RELATIONSHIP VALUE.

I would encourage you to learn all you can about both of these organizations and you will find as I have how MRV can change your business results forever."

Harold Thornton

Harold learned through trial and error that he needed to treat others the way they wanted to be treated, and then he applied this information through personal and social networking.

Most everything we do, we do with others. Since I became proficient at using *The Platinum Rule*, my relationship with my wife has never been better. I have one child who is a Thinker and one who is a Socializer. I have learned to meet them where they are and treat them as they want to be treated. This has resulted in great relationships with my wife and both my children.

I use *The Platinum Rule* in sales and I have learned to identify clients that I enjoy working with. Clients who value me and the services I provide. I created a Business Mastery Advisory Board for business owners and we get great results. This happens because, in the meetings, I treat the members the way they want to be treated. This allows me to ask the question in the way that others want to hear it. It also allows me to challenge them to action in a way they are most receptive to hearing.

Here is an example of how I use *The Platinum Rule*. One of my clients, a small company of 10 people, experienced a serious problem with one of the senior managers. This situation caused everyone to walk out of the company at the same time. I was called and asked to see what I could do to get the company back on track.

I met with the business owner and his daughter, all of the employees, and some of the vendors. The owner was working at the business part time. He was trying to retire. He had his daughter running the day-to-day operations of the business. The owner and the daughter were fighting in front of the employees and a son was waiting in the wings to take over the business when it failed.

I was able to determine that the employees stayed because they really cared for the owner. He was fair, a people person, and he listened when someone wanted his time. The daughter, on the other hand, was handed the business and she did not understand it. She made decisions that were in her best interest and not in the best interests of the company, the employees or the customers. She created rules to make her life easier, not those of the employees or customers. The father was a Director with a strong understanding of people and their needs. The daughter was an extreme Socializer who disliked routine and boredom. The rest of the team were Relaters who cared deeply for the father and the business.

Once we took them through the interview process, training, and the resolution process, they better understood the impact their behavior was having on each other. Some organizational changes were made to better define the day-to-day procedures. An employee handbook was created to clarify company policy. Then the hard work began. Though it was not easy, the company started creating a way for employees to address problems in the organization that would be positively received by others. When I left the organization, people enjoyed their work again, the new policy manual helped create harmony because everyone now understood the rules, and the owner was clear on his exit strategy.

The Platinum Rule is easy to learn and use. The tough part is being persistent enough to use it until it becomes second nature to you. Ask yourself how your life would be different if you knew how to build better and more effective relationships. Would your relationship with your wife or children improve? Could you increase sales and make more money? Could you spend less time addressing people issues because they understood you the first time? How would using The Platinum Rule take you closer to your intelligent self-interest?

Using *The Platinum Rule* benefits you in several ways. Helping other people brings you genuine satisfaction. They benefit from your helpfulness, which in turn inspires them to accept both your personal and your corporate vision. This is a prime example of the win/win philosophy which we identified as your intelligent self-interest, the "good selfishness" as opposed to the "bad selfishness," way back in Chapter One.

What Bill learned using *The Platinum Rule*, he applied in his business and with his family. Over time he became very good in sales because he understood how people wanted to buy. His relationship with his wife and children improved and much of the stress he felt in dealing with others disappeared.

In the next chapter we will discuss persistence. Any time you learn something new your effectiveness will suffer. Persistence is essential to success. Bill will tell you why persistence was important to the conference's success. Read on to find out why.

CHAPTER 6:

THE POWER OF PERSISTENCE

"Many of life's failures are men who did not realize how close they were to success when they gave up."

–Thomas Edison

55

In prior chapters we talked about the importance of intelligent self-interest or selfishness, measuring results, taking ownership, implementing discipline, and treating people the way they want to be treated. Now let's focus on the importance of persistence.

It is hard to be persistent if you do not have any idea why you need to be persistent. Intelligent self-interest is essential to persistence.

Earlier we discussed intelligent self-interest. It is an understanding of what we need to accomplish, taking ownership of our situation, and taking action to get the desire results. Here is why intelligent self-interest (selfishness) is so important.

Here is list of companies who took risks and made mistakes, and as a result of these mistakes they created new products and services:

- Post-it notes from 3M was a mistake

- Ivory soap was a mistake when the operator forgot to turn off the mixer

- The discovery of rubber vulcanization was made by accident

- Levi Strauss made the mistake of selling his entire supply of dry goods leaving him with only canvas to make pants from

- Milton Hershey failed more than once in the candy making business before finding success with the Hershey bar

- Walt Disney filed bankruptcy twice before finding success

Do you think they would have been successful if they were not persistent?

We have a natural tendency to avoid action because trial and error is a frightening thing. Often we find uncertainty to be disquieting. Action is about change and we all know how frightening change can be. Here are some examples of why:

- In 1876, the president of Western Union brushed off Alexander Graham Bell's telephone as little more than an "electric toy," and the company called Bell's proposal to put one in every home "utterly out of the question."

- Oxford University professor Erasmus Wilson predicted that when the 1878 Paris Exhibition closed, the electric light would "close with it and no more will be heard of it."

- A Michigan banker advised his client not to invest in Henry Ford's company in 1903 because "the horse is here to stay, but the automobile is only a novelty."

- Microsoft founder Bill Gates freely admits he was years behind in seeing the promise of the Internet.

When we take inspired action and do not get the desired results, we can consider it a failure. We may consider giving up or we may actually give up. Usually, this happens when we are learning something new and we want results now.

Persistence, according to *Webster's Dictionary*, is the continuance of an effect after the cause is removed. We need to keep trying something until we get the results we want. I call that failing forward.

An example will help. For years I worked as a consultant, redesigning business processes for some of the largest companies in the world. In one situation, we were working with a bank, the Accounts Payables department to be specific, and our goal was to bring the payment processing time down from in excess of 90 days to something under 30 days. Employees were not getting their expenses reimbursed in a timely manner and the bank was losing early payment discounts from vendors because they were missing deadlines, just to name two of the problems we identified.

Prior to us (our team) starting the project, each clerk was paying 75 invoices per day. It was taking on average 90 days for an invoice to be paid. When we completed the project, each clerk was paying between 275 and 325 invoices per day. One clerk actually processed 600 invoices in one day! Invoices were being paid in 24 hours, down from 90 days.

After we installed the new system, productivity dropped from 75 invoices per day per person to between 25 and 50 invoices per day per person. Through persistence, they learned the new systems and productivity increased daily. If the company and the department had given up after we installed the new systems without giving the new actions a chance to fully develop, we would have been a failure.

I have implemented hundreds of these types of application, and it is always the same. When you learn something new, effectiveness actually decreases, until you master the new skills. It is the same in your personal life as well. When you implement a new action, such as a change of diet or exercising regularly, you actually start to feel worse. You are sore from exercising or you might feel hungry until your body adjusts to the new lifestyle. If you stop when the new behavior gets hard, it will be impossible to achieve the desired results. This is where persistence comes into play.

Bill, when he created the conference, made many mistakes in motivating others who were not being paid. He needed to inspire business owners to share what they did well. He needed to sell others to get involved into the conference. Early on this was not a big problem because Bill was the sole representative and people bought into his enthusiasm. As the conference grew Bill had to figure out ways to transfer his knowledge and enthusiasm for the conference so others could do their job. Here are some things Bill learned:

1. Get clear on your selfishness or ISI.

2. Find an accountability partner to help hold you accountable to your ISI.

3. Define the actions needed to achieve your goal.

4. Meet with your accountability partner weekly for 30 minutes. It is a planned meeting with a specific agenda and defined goals.

There is something magical when you choose to hold yourself accountable for your actions and the results you achieve by taking the prescribed actions. This relationship with your accountability coach must be honest and the feedback positive. You do not need to like what you are hearing but be open and know the other person has your best interest at heart, just as you should his. This needs to be a two-way street. Having an accountability partner is not supposed to be a lovefest. It is supposed to be a tool to keep you focused on what you need to achieve and help you break through barriers that hinder your effectiveness.

Bill also suggests you create a habit. Once you measure everything and determine what works, create a measurable, repeatable and predictable process that drives the desired behavior.

Too often we make excuses for not doing what we should. If I want to exercise regularly, I can decide to work out on Monday, Wednesday and Friday. I put it on my schedule as an appointment and I treat it as I would a meeting with a client. I will not miss a meeting with a client; I will not miss a meeting with myself.

For years I mediated for 30 minutes a day. I got away from this practice when I turned the room I used for mediation into an office. I decided I wanted to start again. Every day I get up and the first thing I do is mediate for five minutes. I will expand this time but the important thing is to start.

Finally, Bill suggests we fail more than we succeed. Bill learned the need to reframe failure into something positive. Let's use a rocket as an example. A rocket is always adjusting to ensure it is on target; we need to do the same thing. Most people think a rocket goes from point A to point B without any adjustments. That is not true. A rocket makes thousands of calculations (adjustments) per second. The process goes something like this:

The rocket is fired. It goes through its calculations to find it is off course by three degrees, so it corrects. It finds that it has over-corrected and is now off two degrees in the other direction, so it makes another adjustment. This process goes on until the rocket reaches its goal. The rocket continues to fail forward - toward the end results, the goal, its intelligent self-interest (the destination).

Thomas Edison was once asked by a reported how it felt to fail so many times. Edison told the reporter that he never failed. He told the reporter that if he tried something 10,000 times and it did not work, he did not fail. He simply learned 10,000 ways it did not work.

You need to think like Edison. Do not fail. Just understand that if you try something and you do not get the desired results, learn from your results and try something else; fail forward. Reframe the failure experience into something positive and try again. After all, if your intelligent self-interest is powerful enough, you will be inspired to fail forward. That is why getting clear on your selfishness (intelligent self-interest) is so important. It helps to motivate you and it can keep you motivated when you need to be persistent.

I am of the sincere belief that people fail not because they lack skills. I think they fail because they are not inspired. Because they are not inspired, when they face a difficult situation, instead of failing forward, they give up. They either did not develop their intelligent self-interest or they lost sight of it.

Find your dream, your intelligent self-interest, and be like Thomas Edison. Reframe every negative experience into something positive and stay focused on your intelligent self-interest. Do not let others steal your dream.

There are two types of people in the world today: those who move away from pain and those who go through pain to achieve their intelligent self-interest. When you take action to move away from pain and the pain stops, forward movement stops too. If you stay focused on your intelligent self-interest, you will embrace the actions necessary to achieve your selfishness by moving through the pain. If you are a person who needs pain to move forward, keep yourself in some level of pain to ensure you do not stop moving; don't get comfortable.

I received this quote from a friend after a particularly difficult time. He framed it and presented it to me at a Toastmasters meeting because he admired the work I was doing and the effort it required.

I keep it hanging on my wall as a reminder that persistence is required. It is titled *The Man in the Arena* by President Theodore Roosevelt. Thanks for the support and encouragement Chris. Here it is:

"It is not the critic who counts, nor the man who points out how the strong man stumbled; or where the doer of deeds could have done better. The credit belongs to the man in the arena; whose face is marred by dust and sweat and blood; who strives valiantly; who errs and comes up short again and again; who knows the great enthusiasms, the great devotions, and spends himself in a worthy cause; who at his best, knows the end of triumph of high achievement; and who knows the worst, if he fails, at least fails while daring greatly, so that his place shall never be with those cold and timid souls who know neither victory or defeat."

When I first started writing about different ideas and concepts, especially those documented in this book, I received all kinds of comments. Some of the comments were less than flattering; others were more supportive. It took me a long time to understand that I do not have to let others control what I did (or did not do).

I am not talking about people who offered constructive criticism or made suggestions to improve the work. I value that kind of feedback. It is critical to both personal and business growth. I am talking about the people who were angry and vocal that I would choose to write something they disagreed with; how I stole their dreams and did not care about them. These types of anonymous notes and emails were, at first, discouraging. Then I heard a comment by Dan Kennedy that made sense. I am paraphrasing here.

"Whatever you say will make someone angry. It doesn't matter. Leave them alone and write for the people who want to hear what you have to say."

This next section is for those of you who need some encouragement. I really subscribe to this quote from Calvin Coolidge.

"Nothing in the world can take the place of Persistence. Talent will not; nothing is more common than unsuccessful men with talent. Genius will not; unrewarded genius is almost a proverb. Education will not; the world is full of educated derelicts. Persistence and determination alone are omnipotent. The slogan 'Press On' has solved and always will solve the problems of the human race."

People and companies fail because they give up too soon.

Once they take the time to create their selfishness, take ownership of the situation, and get focused on implementing the disciplines (actions) necessary to be successful, successful people and companies understand that problems will surface. Things never work the way we expect them to work. Successful people keep their eyes clearly fixed on their intelligent self-interest; they are persistent in trying different things to overcome these obstacles. They fail forward and they know where they are going. They know they can't be stopped. They know that their persistence is what drives them forward. They will find a way around any obstacle, and keep right on going. This is persistence.

In the next chapter we will discuss focus, and why focus is so important to persistence and to your selfishness and intelligent self-interest. Focus requires answering two very powerful questions.

CHAPTER 7:

THE POWER OF FOCUS - JUST TWO IMPORTANT QUESTIONS

"Obstacles are those frightful things you see when you take your eyes off your goal."

–Henry Ford

In the prior chapters we talked about the importance of intelligent self-interest or selfishness, measuring results, taking ownership, creating discipline, understanding how to treat others the way they want to be treated, and persistence. Now we will discuss the power of focus.

What Bill realized was what you measure, you focus on. By defining clear roles and responsibilities for the conference volunteers and defining clear outcomes that were measurable, Bill and his team was able to focus on specific outcomes.

One cold winter day, I was attending a basketball game in Cleveland (Cleveland Cavaliers). Before the game there was 13 inches of snow on the ground. Because this was a big game, parking was hard to find so I parked a few blocks away. This was not too bad because the sun was out. The sky was clear but the ground was wet. After the game, as I was walking to the car, I was really focused on where my feet landed because the snow had turned to ice and walking was difficult. Because I did not want to fall, I had my head down and I was watching where I put my feet to avoid twisting an ankle or a knee. Because I was looking down, I almost ran into a police officer who was directing traffic for cars leaving the parking garage.

He looked at me and said (rather sarcastically), "Don't you see the other people waiting?"

I said, "Actually, I didn't. I was watching where I was walking so I did not fall."

When he realized I was not being an idiot and trying to ignore his authority, he was very polite and let me pass.

As a business coach and consultant I realized right then the value of focus. I always knew of and taught about focus, but now I really understood focus.

Focus allows you to stay clear on the desired outcome. It allows you not to be distracted. I was so focused on not falling that I did not see the other people to my right - no more than 5 feet away.

Staying focused is asking yourself only two questions.

These questions take you back to your intelligent self-interest (selfishness).

These questions reinforce the ownership aspect of your decision.

These questions keep you looking at the effectiveness of your actions, the results. The two questions are designed to drive personal accountability. To keep you focused on what is important.

These two questions are:

- Is what I am going taking me closer to my intelligent self-interest?

- If not, why am I doing it?

There is no room to hide here, boys and girls. You either are or you are not.

To paraphrase Yoda in Star Wars: "There is no trying; only doing."

Are you staying focused on what is important to you? If not, why? Did you set your intelligent self-interest too high? Since we are consistently learning, did your intelligent self-interest change? It's ok if it did. Learn from it and fail forward.

When people lose focus, I find two potential challenges are presents. The first is that they lost sight of their intelligent self-interest, they never identified it, or it changed. Two, they are working on things they want to do and not on things they need to be doing.

Let me give you a personal example. I know how important keeping my financial house in order is. Yet it is not something I enjoy doing. I did it grudgingly and it did not get the full attention it deserved. When I realized I did not like the job and was not giving it the attention it deserved, I hired a bookkeeper to perform this function. A simple step to be sure but it allowed me to spend my time doing the things I want and like to do, the activities that take me closer to my intelligent self-interest.

I was coaching a president of a private school and he found his intelligent self-interest. He loved his job and the positive impact he and his organization were having on students. He had one employee who was not happy and her work suffered. He was going to fire her, a very painful decision for him. As we talked about the situation and behavior style of the person involved, I realized she was bored and not doing work in her best interest. Her natural behavioral style was that of a Socializer: outgoing, did not like details, enthusiastic, likes variety. Her current job did not allow her to use her strengths. She was doing, for her, routine, detailed work that kept her tied to her desk. I suggested we allow her to give tours of the school to the parents of prospective students. This president, at first reluctant, agreed to give it a try. It was a good decision. She was so excited about the possibility of doing the tours that her natural enthusiasm emerged and it wasn't long before enrollment started increasing. At this writing, the organization has met all enrollment goals set by the Board of Directors.

By ensuring that people are using their natural skills instead of being forced into a position that the organization needs, an organization can identify, cultivate, and focus on hiring the correct person for the job, thus reducing cost of training and turnover. Again, a win/win situation which is in the best intelligent self-interest of both the organization and its workers, simply by treating its workers the way they wish to be treated.

If we can do this for our employees, it makes sense for us to do it for ourselves as business owners as well. I had a client who loved to create products, solve problems, and build relationships. He built an organization that did not allow him to do that. His business became a prison for him. We trained his entire staff on the principles of *The Platinum Rule* and transformed both him and the company. He transitioned employees to more productive tasks. Effectiveness and efficiency both improved. For example, one critical process took over 90 days to complete. After he empowered people to make changes, the process was automated and process time dropped from over 90 days to only 30 seconds (the process was automated).

The ones who did not buy into the new program left the organization voluntarily. He eventually sold the company and now runs a consulting business that allows him to do what he likes to do, create products and one-page partnerships. His focus has improved because he got clear on his intelligent self-interest and he is doing what he wants to do. He is much happier.

The concept we used to determine this is called *The Platinum Rule*. If you jumped in reading this book and you want to learn more, return to the chapter called *Inspiring Others to Successful Action*.

Remember in our last chapter we discussed failing forward. It took me several tries to get clear on what my intelligent self-interest was all about. It may be the same with you. That is ok. Intelligent self-interest can and will change as you take action. When you take action you will see possibilities that did not exist before. Be flexible.

If you do get distracted or lose sight of your grand plan, that's ok too. Use it as a learning opportunity and get refocused. Do not beat yourself up. Beating yourself up does absolutely no good.

Some of the common problems with losing focus include getting pushed back by those close to you. Are you strong enough to maintain your course and not let others derail you? Is your intelligent self-interest strong enough to help you overcome your challenges? If your intelligent self-interest is not strong enough, I would suggest it may not be the right intelligent self-interest. If is it, surround yourself with people who will see your vision and help you achieve it.

Remember persistence. If you are losing interest, you have not yet found your true intelligent self-interest. Stay true (focused) to your intelligent self-interest.

So how can you become focused and stay focused? It is easy to talk about and hard to implement. Simply put, you must decide what is important to you and stay focused on the desired outcome. Some call it a goal, some call it being focused, some call it tunnel vision, some call it discipline, but you must decide what you want.

There are many systems for setting goals. Jim Rohn, Jack Canfield, and Stephen Covey all discuss systems for setting goals. They discuss the differences between a goal and a dream.

Intelligent self-interest is different from goal setting. Goals must follow your intelligent self-interest. Goals are how you put your intelligent self-interest into action. Let me suggest some things I do and maybe they will help you if you implement them.

1. Get clear on what you want.

67

2. Break your intelligent self-interest down into measurable, actionable steps that have clearly defined completion dates. Writing a book is a good example. Here are some steps that need to be taken: define the topic, create the outline, define the action you will take to fill in each section of the outline, research your ideas, write your draft, rewrite your draft, find an editor, find a publisher and/or an agent, etc. Each of these steps needs clearly defined action steps and completion dates. Writing the book is your intelligent self-interest. The discrete goals for each step turns your intelligent self-interest into a reality.

3. Create a relationship with your accountability partner. Be honest with what you want to accomplish and how you plan to accomplish it. Be open to feedback and change your strategy as required without losing sight of your intelligent self-interest.

4. Create a group of people, your personal advisory board, who you meet with regularly to help you with objective feedback and ideas to move you forward. Provide others with the same objective feedback.

5. Make staying focused on your intelligent self-interest a priority through your accountability partner and your advisory board.

6. Pay someone you can hold accountable to help you achieve success if necessary. Why pay them? Because if they don't perform, you can fire them. Paying someone also helps you be really serious about what you want to accomplish. People do not value something that is free.

How might this apply in business? It is very hard for a company to be focused if it does not know where it is going. The dictionary defines focus as "close or narrow attention; concentration." Without a clear perspective, you cannot focus on the desired outcome. It is too easy to become distracted, disorganized, and inconsistent. When you understand what it is you are to be selfish about, you generate a clear focus, a sense of purpose.

Focus begs an answer to the following questions: Is what I am doing taking me closer to my goal? If not, you must ask yourself why you are doing it. Sometimes we are on the right path but implementing the wrong behavior. Other times we are on the wrong path implementing the right behavior. This is important to understand. People see your commitment, your focus, and your passion. If your behavior is not aligned with your belief systems, you can do all the right things and still not achieve your selfishness.

If the specific behavior is not allowing you to focus on what is important, you must make a decision. The decision is simple: Do I keep this behavior understanding it is not helping me achieve my goal?

A simple example might help. Let us assume you are a sales representative and you do not get paid unless you sell. In business we call this eating what you kill. You do not kill, you do not eat. If you are afraid to pick up the telephone and make a call to someone who might become a customer, it will be hard to create success. You have two choices: learn to pick up the phone or partner with someone who can do this for you.

Some steps you can take include visualizing daily the act of picking up the phone and making your calls. Then do it. Take two minutes every day and see yourself performing the very activities you know you need to do but are not doing. Over time you will naturally perform this activity because you have already performed it over and over in your mind.

Create a clear picture and visualize the outcome of the phone call. Feel what it is like when you experience the ideal phone call. Feel grateful, and then get busy.

Here is an example of how I use gratitude to maintain focus and discipline. When gas reached four dollars a gallon, I really tried to watch my driving habits. I was reluctant to pull into a gas station and buy gas. I decided I'd had enough of this mindset, and every time I purchased gas I realized how grateful I was to be able to afford to buy this gas. I reframed buying gas from a painful experience to one of gratitude. Buying gas no longer hurts.

Focus on your specific goals by doing at least one thing that will take you closer to your intelligent self-interest daily.

Remember to stay well rounded. Focus can and should include different aspects of what is important. Your intelligent self-interest should include: spiritual selfishness, financial self-interest, relationships, and health objectives. Define how others can help you and do not be afraid to ask for help. Ask them how you can help them. Focus on how family can contribute to your goal through support, love, and inspiration. They want you to be successful.

When I was transitioning from an employee in the corporate world to a business owner, my wife was instrumental in helping with this transition. She learned new skills and did things she never thought she could or would do. We both benefited from her change. She became more focused, dynamic and inspired because she was working on things important to her. She learned to run high-end computerized sewing machines and became proficient at selling them. She became a seamstress and created costumes for the Ohio Ballet (and others); she created new, valuable relationships, all with the intent of accomplishing her intelligent self-interest.

This is important because your behavior will positively or negatively impact those around you. Nothing happens in a vacuum. This can be either a source of nourishment or difficulties in a relationship. Know this: as you embrace these principles, your existing relationships will change. Be gentle with them and with yourself as you redefine the relationship.

Here as some things you can do to help you get and stay focused.

1. Do a behavioral assessment that will help you understand both your strengths and weaknesses.

2. Analyze the results of the assessment with what you are actually doing in your business or your daily work activities.

3. Create a plan that will allow you to spend more time on what you do well and less time on what you do not like to do.

4. Do the things you do not like to do first so you can quickly move into the fun areas of your day.

5. Ask yourself: Is what I am doing taking me towards my intelligent self-interest? If not, why am I doing it? If it needs to be done, can it be outsourced, delegated, or otherwise effectively removed from your plate?

Bill and his team had monthly one-hour conference calls for 10 months prior to the next conference. Two months before the conference, these calls were held every two weeks. These calls kept people focused.

In the next chapter we will discuss ideas. This is a big problem for most people. The problem is not lack of ideas; it is too many ideas.

CHAPTER 8:

TOO MANY IDEAS? NOT ENOUGH IDEAS? WHAT IS ONE TO DO?

"This is my answer to the gap between ideas and action - I will write it out."

–Hortense Calisher

73

In the previous chapter we talked about the importance of intelligent self-interest or selfishness, measuring results, taking ownership, developing discipline (habits), understand how to treat others the way they want to be treated, being persistent, and staying focused. Let's address the concepts of ideas and why they are important and how they can both help and hinder us.

Once we decide on our intelligent self-interest and determine a course of action, we can run into one of two problems: too many ideas or not enough ideas. How do we take our selfishness, our intelligent self-interest, and figure out how to turn it into a reality? How do we solve this dilemma?

As Bill and his team worked on the conference, their discussion and focus was on creating an outstanding conference that other business owners found valuable. Bill and his team discussed many ideas and over time the ideas were vetted and dismissed or assigned to someone to work through. Each meeting, they got more and more focused on fewer and fewer ideas. As they implemented the ideas, the focused changed to refining and improving the conference. This group of volunteers acted as an advisory board to ensure the correct decisions were made and implemented.

How can you get clear on the best ideas for you?

Let me tell you specifically what I do and have done to transform my life and my business.

I created a concept call Business Mastery Advisory Board (www.rpfgroupinc.com).

This board is composed of other like-minded people who are dedicated to providing intelligent and objective feedback, practical suggestions, usable advice and best practices to help me get results.

It does three things for me:

1. Keeps me focused on my intelligent self-interest

2. Provides concrete ideas (objective feedback) to take me deeper into achieving my intelligent self-interest

3. Holds me accountable to help me eliminate the ideas that seemed good at the time but have no real value and take me away from what is important

Is it easy putting your dreams and goals out for others to see? No, it is not. It can be quite scary. Once you put it out there, there is no place to hide.

Is it important? You better believe it.

Many times we do not achieve our goals because we do not know how, especially in this day and age where it is impossible to keep up with the dynamic pace of change.

If you do not share your intelligent self-interest, how will you find someone to help you? If you do not share your intelligent self-interest, then you have not taken ownership. If you do not share your intelligent self-interest, how can you create an advisory board of like-minded people to help you?

I know what you are thinking. I do not need an advisory board, I can do it myself. Good luck! Every major company has a board. They call theirs a Board of Directors. The Board of Directors is tasked with holding the senior management team accountable to achieving the plan. They help clear out obstacles. They help with objective feedback, practical advice, and best practices.

If they use the concept, doesn't make sense for you to do the same thing?

You do not have to go it alone. You do not want to go it alone. Find a board of trusted advisors and hold each other responsible to help you achieve the intelligent self-interest that is so important to you.

Take action now!

In the next chapter we will discuss action in more detail. I will let you in on a secret. The real definition of success is action. You are making great progress; keep going. The next chapter is the heart of the book.

CHAPTER 9:

A NEW DEFINITION OF SUCCESS IS ....

"When I was kidnapped, my parents snapped into action. They rented out my room."

–Woody Allen

We have talked about the importance of intelligent self-interest or selfishness, results, ownership, discipline, people, persistence, staying focused, and ideas. All the previous chapters just served to set up this chapter on success.

What does success mean to you?

For Bill, success was defined as having 300 paid attendees at the conference. Did he succeed? Yes he did. He knew that running a successful conference required taking action to get thing done. Specifically activities that allowed the conference attendees to grow, flourish and get results.

I do over 100 talks a year on business mastery and success. In almost every talk I ask this question. "What does success mean to you?" If there are 100 people in the room I will get 95 different answers. The answers include:

- "Being happy."

- "Making more money."

- "More family time."

- "Financial freedom."

- "Personal freedom."

- "Better relationships."

- "Less stress."

The list goes on.

How can the word "success" have so many different meanings? If we cannot agree on a meaning how can we communicate it effectively?

As you have probably gathered by now, if you cannot define something you cannot achieve it. I will ask the audience "What does being happy mean?", "What does making more money mean?", or "What does freedom mean?" If you cannot define it you cannot achieve it. Many times they cannot define what more freedom means, or what more money means. Does more money mean having enough to eat out when you want to? Does it mean being able to pay for your children's college? Does it mean having a great retirement, a new home, or better clothes?

I finally realized people confuse the outcomes of success with being successful.

Let me say that again. I finally realized people confuse the outcomes of success with being successful.

Let me explain.

If you have the Oxford Dictionary of Word History, take a minute to look up the word "success." When the word was introduced into the English language, it simply met to achieve. There was no moral judgment. If I stole something, I was as successful as someone who built a house.

I then looked up the word "achieve" in the same dictionary. The dictionary gave the definition as "taking action."

I finally realized that success simply means to take action; taking action on your intelligent self-interest, your selfishness. The outcomes of being successful (take action) are:

- "Being happy."

- "Making more money."

- "More family time."

- "Financial freedom."

- "Personal freedom."

- "Better relationships."

- "Less stress."

- Etc.

If success means to take action, what action do you need to take to achieve your intelligent self-interest? After all, your intelligent self-interest is what you defined as success.

In the previous chapters I laid out the nine actions successful people implement. Let me review them here:

1. Intelligent Self-Interest (selfishness)

2. Taking Ownership

3. Measuring Everything - Results

4. Understanding People

5. Being Persistent

6. Staying Focus

7. Creating habits - Discipline

8. Creating Ideas

9. Taking action

Create or join your own Business Mastery Advisory Board (www. rpfgroupinc.com). This board needs to be composed of other like-minded people who are dedicated to providing intelligent and objective feedback, practical suggestions, usable advice, and best practices to help YOU get results.

Success is action! Take action now!

CHAPTER 10:

USING THIS KNOWLEDGE EVERY DAY

"Knowledge without action is useless."

–Ron Finklestein

Let me take a minute to introduce Robert Schepens. Robert is the president of two very successful companies, but that was not always the case.

I met Robert at a business conference that invited business owners to tell what they did right. The intent of the conference was to showcase successful companies and have them do a 30-minute presentation on what they did right. The conference founders wanted to transfer knowledge to the conference attendees so they could do the same actions to grow their business. Because I did consulting for Fortune 1000 companies for over 20 years, I knew "right action" when I saw it. The judges (I was not one) also saw the value and selected Robert's company as the winner the year he entered. That is how I met Robert (I call him Bob).

Over the years the conference founders received hundreds of nominations (that is how I distilled these nine principles). As Bob and I got to know each other we realized we had much in common: helping others to grow personally and professionally. We shared war stories and helped each other when called upon.

I want to stress I had no involvement with Bob and Champion Staffing as he transformed his company. Bob is a very smart man. In addition to his native intelligence, Bob understands the value of feedback from others. He belongs to one of my advisory boards (and frankly he gives more than he gets back) and he takes what he learns from others and applies it in ways specific to his ISI.

I asked Bob to write this chapter because he reflects the nine principles and how living them can transform both a company and a life. As you read you will find he had to fire his father from the business and take specific action based on his specific ISI to save a company. I don't want to steal Bob's story so let me introduce to you Robert Schepens, my good friend and mentor. It was through his guidance that this book took its current form and I learned so much about him.

First, allow me an ethical and cultural prelude to my story.

"Akita Mani Yo" in the Lakota-Sioux language translates loosely to "Observe everything as you walk your path in life." Be acutely aware of your surroundings, how you react to them, how they react to you and the impact you are having on all things and people around you. It is a positioning directive, an Ethos. It is in fact the "Intelligent" part of "Intelligent Self-Interest."

As an admonition, Akita Mani Yo or Observe Everything As You Walk can be followed by another phrase of Native Wisdom: "Mitakuye Oyasin" (Lakota-Sioux), "We are all related" (everything is connected).

In the Native American culture, these phrases are principles in action that have been passed down for generations from before the first visitors to this land, to teach character and a way of life to each generation. They teach how to be strong, how to be a good warrior by being in touch with (sensitive to) everything.

Combine the two phrases and we have a simple directive for success in life or commerce: "Take everything and everyone into consideration as you choose the path to your goals, as your actions are connected to everything and everyone."

Furthermore, the observations of the real world reduce the ability to rationalize one's actions as they provide factual feedback of the consequences to those actions. The observations provide accountability (ownership) for those actions.

All rolled up: Intelligent Self-Interest: A Foundation for the 9 Principles of Success.

None of us incorporates all 9 Principles in perfect harmony. But each of us can have a hierarchy of those principles that work for us. Mine begins with Intelligent Self-Interest as defined by both Akita Mani Yo and Mitakuye Oyasin.

The 9 Principles in action:

I rescued my main company from another owner in 1995, when it had one office and about seven people, and was close to being out of business. While my father was ill and away from the business, other people ran the company into the ground in selfish ways. So selfish were those intentions that those people did not and still do not believe they were wrong.

The company has now grown to seven offices, 40 employees (including an extraordinarily innovative spinoff organization called A Job Near Home), and along the way we have accumulated an incredible number of business achievement awards, certifications and accolades. As a matter of fact, no other company in our profession, in our region, has achieved what we have. That includes a "Reinvention Period" where we TOTALLY changed the nature of the services we offered. Totally.

Importantly, we have also been recognized as one of the top 99 companies to work for in all of North East Ohio (North Coast 99 in 2007, 2008 and hopefully many more years). And we are the fourth smallest company on that list. We are considered just as good a place to work as companies that employ thousands of people. (#4 in action: Inspiring other people to accept personal and corporate visions.)

How? Before the 9 Principles were defined I had learned my version of Intelligent Self-Interest from an Indian Brother, as defined above. Even though it is ingrained in my genetics, it has not been easy to follow. Nothing of value is easy. It is a constant battle between doing the right things in the right way and doing things that are focused on oneself or only on other people. Everything we have done in our business has been with ISI in mind: being aware of Akita Mani Yo: Considering everything and everyone that our actions can touch. After all, we are in fact connected to everyone and everything we touch. We have an ancestral command to take that into consideration.

My ISI has been to create a sustainable, high performance company that would challenge all employees to perform at their peak and to perform for our clients at a level no other firm could. A company with value and of values. A company that would take the best from our employees and in turn give the best we could offer back to them.

Initially, the rescue of the business took substantial (philosophical, strategic and personal) risk, a tremendous focus in the face of naysayers, and the taking of actions necessary to simply keep the platform alive. (Three of the nine principles right there.) My beginning ISI was simple: I had to keep the company alive while earning break even and be able to pay the previous owner a reasonable and dignified retirement. My father's livelihood was a real and philosophic priority. He got paid first, then the staff, then the vendors, then taxes, and then me. For the first nine months or so everyone got paid. My job was to wait. America! Land of the ever-flowing "you're pre-qualified!" credit cards.

I also had to take action on things that COULD have gotten in the way of my ISI. Phase one of my ISI was to get the company going so I could provide an income to my father. In my naiveté, I had allowed (he demanded) my dad to stay on part time in a subordinate role to give him something to do and potentially to help me. His presence became a complete distraction to my being able to run the company effectively, and with much trepidation I had to let him go ("Dad, You're Fired," Plain Dealer article October 2007).

The sale of the company had not been completed and he threatened to take it back if I did not achieve HIS idea of a level of success in very short order. Unfortunately, he walked on his final journey before we had a chance to formalize the entire sale, and a stepbrother then threw more nails on my path in the way of estate manipulations. Typically, in an estate one would think that the only blood relative of the deceased should get some residual, at least that provided for in a will. I did... a bill for $50,000. I actually had to pay the estate, not have the estate pay me. I did not have the cash, so the step-thief allowed me to pay in installments (he didn't really need the dough I guess) until I was late on a payment that happened to coincide with the 9.11.01 Terrorist attacks. I honestly had other things on my mind at the time, as in "Will my business survive so I can meet payroll?" The step-thief had the note called in by a lawyer who would not even negotiate, and collected lawyer's fees, court fees, late fees and so on. I found the money, paid off everyone, and warned my step-thief to never run across me in a private place with no one else around.

For my goal "One-B" I vowed never to let the management of the company become a whim or a "personal style" of anyone. That had happened when my dad was away from the company: two totally self-serving people were left to run the organization as they saw fit, neither having any "ownership" (real or philosophical) in it nor any need to keep the organization alive. One left before my father or I could return and the other left shortly after I arrived (thank goodness). That one has been with about 12 companies since then, but has maintained a "facade" of success. It is interesting that both resented having ownership return, even though neither had done anything to stop the ship from sinking. I feel sorry for both.

To accomplish "sustainability" and to take the company away from "Management By Whim" to a meaningful systematic approach, we created and implemented an ISO 9001:2000 Quality System at a very high financial and time cost. This assured that regardless of how large (or small) we got, the same system of operation would be used for all our clients and for our own people in all offices, by all people. We appointed a Corporate Quality Manager who is in charge of all operations and has the authority to assure their success. We over-appointed a quality team, and gave them power and authority. This, in essence, accomplished #3 Measuring, #6 Discipline, and #7 Persistence (the ISO Quality System took over one year to install and requires quarterly/annual audits and client surveys). It also gave us a minor sales point in our industry, as only 0.1% (point one) of all staffing firms in the world are ISO certified, all offices. As a side note, in the five years we have been certified, our audits have all been "perfect."

This ISO system essentially created an operating system so that we could have each branch office function in all ways exactly like the others. We simultaneously implemented a system that has ALL offices functioning as though they are one, with daily live conference calls and an internal real-time system of updating and communicating. (#4 Inspiring, #6 Discipline, #8 Surrounding yourself with people and resources; and #3 Measuring all results, #5 Staying focused on what works, #9 Taking Action, and #2 Getting people to take ownership.)

We also implemented our own internal training system that now boasts over 90 hours of in-house produced training DVDs on every topic imaginable to our business. These insure that all people know the same thing about each component of our business. This is critical when you are expanding from one branch office to seven and more in the future. It also speaks to caring about the people you work with and their careers. We give them every opportunity to be successful. And last it assures that "management" is more about consistency than whim. Our people like that. It means stability.

Our internal systems and our legacy of ethical business operations lead into our ability to "inspire people" on our missions. We don't need cheerleaders (although it helps) and we don't need to make things up. We are what our people and customers see, feel and hear 100% of each day. This is a difficult road. But we have chosen to be emotionally stable rather than a rah-rah company.

With our decent profits we provide our staff with an incredible benefit plan that also has an emphasis on being healthy (we have our own fitness center and FAMILY fitness memberships for suburban office folks, health screenings, tobacco cessation, nutrition, weight loss), volunteering, charitable works matching, and some very unique programs like Hybrid Purchase Assistance. (#2 I take ownership in everything we do, #4 Inspiring People, #8 Our ability to hire and surround ourselves with good people, #5 Staying focused on what is important: the people who get us where we want to go).

As our #1 Charitable act, we became the ONLY Drug Free Level II Staffing Service in the entire State of Ohio, certified by the OBWC. And to date, we have educated over 100,000 workers on why drugs and booze are bad things to mix with work. More than all the federal, state and large company employees educated in Ohio, combined. Yes, it saved us money and accidents. But we did it for one true reason: It was the RIGHT thing to do. We are able to do it. Was it, and is it, easy? Absolutely NOT. Even the State of Ohio Bureau of Workers' Compensation has tried to get in our way. Our Zero Tolerance policy was TOO restrictive for OBWC. They wanted a drug free workplace, "kinda." Champion doesn't do "kinda" real well. We have maintained the zero tolerance policy. Now, it is with their blessing.

Were we able to do all this at once? Was it easy? Not even close. There were many, many times I seriously doubted what I was doing, how we were doing it, and if we could handle it financially and emotionally. There were many people in our early years who quit and were HOPING to see us fail (some even tried to help us fail). Only one of those many people who wished us poor business is now "successful."

What we did, however, is simply concentrated on the bigger picture of our goals (ISI) and kept "Akita Mani Yo" in mind: I watched, adjusted, fell back, moved forward...all while keeping our self-interest in mind. I allowed my surroundings to tell me how we were doing and to tell me to keep my ISI in check. I know in many ways I have failed that admonition on a regular basis. It is extraordinarily difficult to live in the modern and ancestral worlds simultaneously. Doing so keeps me and our entire organization honest, keeps us from taking greedy shortcuts and allows us to REALLY sleep at night.

We still have a way to go and are just thankful to be where we are, when many good organizations have failed. AHO! Mitakuye Oyasin! We are all (people, critters, environment and things) connected! If our entire region, country and world would seriously recognize that as a fact of life, our entire world would be much better off. Greed would be replaced by acts of the heart and conscience, and selfishness would be replaced by all of us, not just one of us. If the planet is to see another century, we need to understand that all of us working together is smarter and more effective than one of us walking alone.

Listen to what I have told you. I learned it from people much smarter than I. Now I pass it on to you and maybe you can pass it on to others. If you don't want to listen to me, or Ron, then perhaps you will listen to your own ancestors. Listening shows that you understand the true meaning of Intelligent Self-Interest. Hecetu Yelo (I have spoken). Wopila (that one you have to find on your own).

CHAPTER 11:

DEFINING YOUR INTELLIGENT SELF-INTEREST

"My mother said I must always be intolerant of ignorance but understanding of illiteracy. That some people, unable to go to school, were more educated and more intelligent than college professors."

–Maya Angelou

As we move through this process, please keep a couple of things in mind. Many people don't do this exercise because they are afraid they are going to be wrong. Understand that as you grow you might redefine your desired outcomes and goals. That's ok. Very few of us know what we want from the start, but once we get started the ways will become clear. Here are a few suggestions for your consideration:

- Don't fret it if you have some difficulty; this is a process not a destination.

- If you know what life you want, use this process as a refresher to reaffirm your past decisions and to refocus on the life you would like to live.

- Revisit this process often. As you grow and change it is likely your goals and outcomes will change with you.

- Don't worry about making a mistake - there are no mistakes. As you grow it is not uncommon for you to change what you do and how you do it. The very act of growing can refine and clarify your decisions. People sometimes assume that the decisions they made in college cannot be changed. Not only can they be changed but they should be changed if they no longer work for you. You have changed, you are more mature, and you have a better understanding of what is important to you. Use this knowledge effectively by following the process below.

Your business success is directly related to your personal growth, your ability to eliminate self-limiting and defeating beliefs and replace them with the empowering attitudes and actions of successful people.

I had a defining moment - the loss of a job. I spent many months looking for work and came to the realization that I would have to leave the city I called home to find work. I was not happy about that but being a pragmatist, I would do what needed to be done, I thought.

I spoke with my wife and we decided it was time to relocate. We have two children, and one was still in her second year of high school. We agreed that our daughter would finish school, and she (and my wife) would join me wherever I found a job. When we talked with my daughter, I explained the situation and told her she could finish high school, and then she could join me wherever I landed.

About a week after our discussion, my daughter came back to me and told me that she could graduate high school a year early if she went to summer school. She was the captain of the junior varsity soccer team, in Character Counts and the Latin Club, and was generally having fun enjoying the high school experience. I asked her why she would give all that up. Her answer was honest and simple and it changed my life. She said "I do not want to be away from you for two years."

At that time I made four decisions:

- My problems are not my children's problems.

- I have great skills. I immediately hired myself and started my company, though I was not sure what this meant or where it would lead me.

- We would not have to leave our home after all.

- It was time to give something back to the community.

When I took myself through the process I had laid out, I realized there were four things I wanted:

- Personal freedom

- Financial freedom

- Control over my destiny (no longer would I be in someone's else control)

- When I looked back over my life, I wanted to know that it had some meaning in the bigger scheme of things

This defining moment had been years in the making and was the catalyst I needed for personal and professional change. I realized that what I really wanted was to feel like I had made a contribution to others (I specifically excluded my family) and that my life was not wasted. I could not say I had achieved that. So I asked myself this question. "I am 85 years old and I am on my death bed. What must I accomplish before I die?" In answering that question I realized that my life is short (when I did this exercise I was 50 years old) and I wanted to do something that would allow me to use the two things I most enjoyed: personal growth and teaching.

91

I combined the two most important things in my life, teaching and personal growth, and created a business coaching and consulting company, AKRIS INC. That is how this book was born and the training program created. The process you are about to experience is the direct result of the process of I went through to start, build and grow my company.

Let's start with understanding what kind of life you want. Washington Irving said it best when he said: "Great minds have purpose. Others have wishes." I needed to find my purpose, my intelligent self-interest, my selfishness. Here is how I did that.

I realized I needed something bigger in my life. Something that would provide meaning. I asked myself these questions:

- Why is a life purpose important?

- How can I creating a life's vision and mission to support that purpose?

- What action steps can I take to implement this vision and mission?

- How does this purpose relate directly to my success?

Reason for a Life Purpose

Successful people cannot be focused, disciplined, persistent, responsible, results oriented, ownership-driven and selfish without a clear purpose of where they want to go and what they want to achieve. A personal vision and mission drive the implementation of a life's purpose. I used them to create a successful business. If you decide owning a business is not for you, don't despair. These same steps can be used, but you must understand that you still need to be focused, disciplined, persistent, responsible, results oriented, ownership-driven and selfish in your chosen lifestyle.

How will your work/job/business help you create the life you want? How do you know what you want?

How Do You Know Your Personal Vision?

For our purposes we will stay focused on how your personal vision will help you succeed. If you are not clear about what your personal vision is, watch your:

- Unguarded thoughts

- Intuition (what feels right)

- Inklings (something that leads us in an unexpected direction)

- Daydreams

- Hobbies

Write them down. Something magical happens when you write it down. It's like telling your conscious mind you are serious. When you pay attention, subtle things will take you in directions you never thought possible. It has been my experience that we know what is in our best interest if we can get out of our own way.

Here is a real example from my life. Ten years ago I had a daydream of writing a book. I had no clue what it would be about and I never knew what topic to choose. More importantly I never felt I had anything worthwhile to say. I dismissed it as an idle daydream that would never happen. This daydream came back; it never left me alone but I refused to acknowledge it.

When I started a business conference, I did research on the 41 companies who participated. I realized they all did the same things. I was speaking to a friend of mine and sharing my findings with her. She said, "You sound just like Michael Gerber, you should write a book."

I now had the topic, the material and the interest in taking this daydream and making it a reality. Since that time, I have written (including this one) four books and contributed to several others. At the time I decided to write the book, I had no clue how to organize or write a book. Now I not only write books, I publish them as well.

Why a Personal Vision Is So Important

Everyone needs a personal vision to live by and goals that will help you understand:

- Supporting your life's purpose

- When to decide to do something

- How to do it

- Why to do it

- How to stay motivated to get through the tough times

In going through this process, I clarified three things that were important to me: honesty, integrity and common sense. I define honesty as always speaking from the heart, the truth as I see it. Integrity is doing what I tell you I am going to do. Common sense means I do something if it makes sense for all parties involved, a win/win for everyone involved. If a decision does not meet those three criteria I don't do it. This makes my life so simple.

What is Personal Vision?

Every high achiever knows how taking action will support them to create the life they want once they define what they want. They have the attitude that their business is only a tool to help create the life they want. As a result, they develop a "vision" about how their career supports them in creating this ideal life.

Their Personal Vision Statement guides them. They know that every action is taking them where they want to go. They take charge. They take full responsibility for defining and fulfilling their vision regardless of market conditions, their co-workers' griping or their current level of compensation. They realize that they can't wait until external factors, like the marketplace, get better ... but that THEY must get better if they intend to achieve their goals.

A personal vision is a mental picture, an image or concept held in the mind. It is also the ability to anticipate possible future events and developments. I like to think of personal vision as something that I will never achieve, but more the image I want others to see.

A Personal Vision Statement is:

- Something that you keep handy (a handwritten or typed paragraph or a dream board posted some place you can see it regularly)

- Committed to memory

- A long term vision of what you want to create; you understand that it may not be attainable but it inspires you to continue moving forward

My personal vision statement is quite simple: educate, motivate and influence business owners to take inspired action that leads to successful results. Here's a process you can use right now to create a personal vision statement for your personal success.

Personal Vision Exercise: Take 10 minutes to develop a story of how your business will help you create the life you want. Define what you want. Do you want:

- Money (why?) and how much

- Control (of what?)

- Freedom (what kind?)

- Prestige (how do you define this?)

- Loving relationships (how do you define this?)

- Respect (how do you define this?)

- Material Possessions (how would they motivate you?)

The SOAR process

SOAR stands for Situation, Opportunity, Action, Results. It is designed to force discipline in the thinking process and create a standard communication process that all will use. It will allow fellow BMAB members to focus on what is being said and not how it is being said.

1. S - Situation. What is the situation (challenge/opportunity) and why is it important? This sets the context for the situation.

2. O - Opportunity. What is the opportunity? What are the expected outcomes if you solve this problem or embrace this opportunity? Focus on the expected results when action is taken on this

particular opportunity.

3.   A - Action. What action did you already take? What were the results? What actions are you planning to take? What are the intended and expected results?

4.   R - Results. What results are you expecting by taking the action defined above?

Go through the SOAR process five times and write down up to five outcomes you want to achieve in your life. Try to mention the things money can buy (if that is important to you) such as a house, car, dream vacation, or working only 20 hours a week. Some of the things that are important to the author include: creating my own security, having enough control over my life to work when I want, knowing when my time on Earth is over that my life has meaning, and not having my children's children pay for their school loans.

List your five top outcomes here:

1. _____

2. _____

3. _____

4. _____

5. _____

For the items you listed above, describe how you will express each characteristic in your career. Start by using the word "by" to begin each phrase. For example, if you listed "create my own security" above, you might write "by making enough in my own business to never have to worry about money." Another example: if you wrote "having control to work when I want" above, you might write "by creating rewarding and satisfying work that allows me work when I want." Write down your desired outcomes you want to experience.

List your positive experiences here:

1. _____

2. _____

3. _____

4. _____

5. _____

For example, my top outcomes included financial security and control over how I achieve that. My first outcome was financial security. The positive experience would be never worrying about money again. My second outcome was to have control over how I achieved this financial freedom and the positive outcome was creating passive forms of income.

Look back over the previous two steps and circle the three most important items in each step. List them here:

Top 3 Outcomes   Top 3 Positive Experiences

_____   _____

_____   _____

_____   _____

Now fill in the blanks of the following paragraph: My personal vision is to....

When finished, you will have a short paragraph that reads something like this: "My vision is to create my own security through the creation of work that is rewarding and satisfying. This work allows me to work when I want, provides the income I desire, and ensures my life has meaning to my clients, friends, family and associates."

My vision is to _____

_____

_____

Now that we know what kind of life you want to create, let's convert the vision statement into a mission statement. The mission statement is the first step in defining how you will implement your vision statement.

Create a Personal Mission

A personal mission is an aim or task that you believe is your duty to carry out or to which you attach special importance and devote special care. It builds on what you defined in your vision by helping you begin implementing the vision you created above.

A mission is a handwritten or typed paragraph posted some place you can see it regularly, such as on a dream board or any other place that makes the mission visible and real to you. I like to think of my mission as my plan to implement my vision.

Here's a process you can use right now to create a Mission Statement for success in your career or business. Take the vision described above and write down all goals that apply to your vision statement. In the above vision statement the author used the example: "create my own security through the creation of work that is rewarding and satisfying." If you want to create your own security, define what that means in concrete, specific terms. For example, security could mean an income such as:

- $10k per month

- 6 months' cash in the bank

- Work you enjoy

- A passive income stream of X dollars a month

For the second part of that sentence, "through the creation of work that is rewarding and satisfying," how do you define rewarding and satisfying? If you can't define rewarding and satisfying, how do you know what you must to do to find rewarding and satisfying work? How do you know that you are making progress towards your desired outcome?

I define rewarding and satisfying as teaching people the skills necessary to achieve and exceed their goals. This could lead to a whole list of products and services.

Another part of the above vision statement is, "This work allows me to work when I want, provides the income I desire, and ensures my life has meaning to my clients, friends, family and associates."

"To work when I want and provide the income I desire," I would create a specific goal. Passive income would allow me to work when I want. Then the question becomes what kind of passive income. I might write something like:

- $10k monthly cash flow from real estate

- $10K a month from online products and services

- The balance will be made up of consulting and speaking engagements that I want to do

- Write and publish a book

To ensure "my life to have meaning," I wrote "I will give back to the community by:

- Creating a business conference and celebrating the successes of others

- Using the knowledge I learn from running the conference to make quality business training available to everyone who wants it

- Setting up an account to pay off my children's college loans and pay for my grandchildren's college educations."

Remember, those are only examples. Please make this specific to your situation.

An example mission statement would read, "My mission is to create the life I want by creating multiple streams of income, creating a company that will give me the freedom to work when I want, and giving back to the community by creating a success conference that enriches my life and the lives of everyone I touch. I will also create a way to provide quality business education to anyone who wants to improve their life by starting their own business."

That has changed for me over the years and now reads "...by teaching others the nine actions successful people implement daily."

Now take your mission statement and become more specific. Write down your mission:

_____

_____

_____

_____

_____

Let's take the next step by turning your mission into specific goals with concrete outcomes. Goals are so misunderstood, yet so important. Goals are nothing more than the place you want to go and when you will get there. To follow Steven Covey's advice on goal setting, goals need to be time bound, realistic, achievable, results oriented and measurable.

To begin, take your outcomes you defined in your mission statement and write them here. Before you do that, be sure you understand what a goal is and what constitutes a good goal.

Good goals are:

- Time Bound: It has a date in which the goal is to be achieved.

- Specific: A good goal must have specific details.

- Measurable: All goals must be measurable. "I will achieve $1,000 in sales by February 10, 2008" is an achievable, realistic, time bound, results oriented and measurable goal.

- Achievable: Can it be achieved? By achievable I mean something you can and want to achieve. For example, I know that I could get a job as a manager doing information technology consulting, but I don't want to, so I won't try to achieve it. This goal is realistic, but for me it is not achievable.

- Realistic: It must be something that you can realistically accomplish. An unrealistic goal for me would be to become a trusted advisor to Bill Gates.

You must be very careful with realistic and achievable when you are setting goals. Our life would be very different if someone had told Thomas Edison that creating the light bulb was not realistic or achievable and he had believed them.

The next component of a good goal is that it must be Results Oriented: Is there a distinct result to this goal? "I want to make $1,000 this week" is a results oriented goal. "I want to make some money to buy a car" is not a results oriented goal. It does not talk about how much money, the type of car, or when this will happen.

On the next page, list your goals that you defined from your vision/mission process above and ask yourself the listed questions about each goal.

(I left room for you to define up to five goals, but do not be constrained by this. Use as many (or few) as needed.)

Goal Description is a brief description of what you want to accomplish. Time bound is the date you expect it to be completed. Realistic is either a yes or no; it is realistic or it is not. Achievable is either a yes or no; it is achievable or it is not. Finally, measurable is either a yes or no; it is measurable or it is not. Make a note under measurable on how you plan to measure the results.

Here is an example. Using the mission statement described above, I wrote "multiple streams of income, creating a company that will give me the freedom to work when I want, and giving back to the community by creating a success conference that enriches my life and the lives of everyone I touch. I will also create a way to provide quality business education to anyone who wants to improve their life by starting their own business."

Let's break this down a bit further. "Multiple streams of income (what does that mean, and what form will it take?), creating a company that will give me the freedom (how do I define this?) to work when I want (how will I define this?), and giving back to the community by creating a success conference that enriches my life and the lives of everyone I touch (what form will this take and when will it be implemented?). I will also create a way to provide quality business education to anyone (how and when?) who wants to improve their life by starting their own business."

Goals Description	Is It Specific? (Yes or No)	What is the Completion Date?	Is it Realistic? (Yes or No)	Is it Achievable? (Yes or No)	Outcomes You Will Experience?
1. Consulting: Define three forms of income.	Yes	Consulting products by 12-31-04	Consulting – Yes	Consulting Products – Yes	Three products defined and tested
2. Take a course in real estate.	Yes	Real estate course by 12-01-06	Real Estate – Yes	Real Estate – Yes	Find a mentor who I can call with questions
3. Take a course in stock investing.	Yes	Stock course by 12-10-07	Stock Course – Yes	Stock Course – Yes	Successful completion of course
4. Write a book on success by 12/31/08.	Yes	Book completed by 12-31-08	Book – Yes	Book – Yes	Published

Using the format above, write and test your goals. Define as many goals as necessary to begin the process of implementing your mission statement.

Goals Description	Is It Specific? (Yes or No)	What is the Completion Date?	Is it Realistic? (Yes or No)	Is it Achievable? (Yes or No)	Outcomes You Will Experience?

Goal Busting Process - Testing and Breaking Through, and Barrier to Your Goal (Barrier Busters Process)

In this step we are going to define any barriers that might prevent you from meeting your goal. We'll also provide a vehicle to eliminate them. (Some of this material is from Kevin Hogan's *The Psychology of Persuasion*.) I will walk through an example for you.

Using the goal described above, "Write and publish a book on business success by December 31, 2008," there are several barriers that would make this a difficult goal to achieve.

What are the reasons I might not be able to achieve this goal? Two immediate problems are finding the time and gathering the information to write this book.

Let's address the problem of finding the time first. What is the pain I will experience if I do not find the time to write the book? The pain is that I will not move forward on creating the financial freedom goal or creating passive income, and the disappointment I will feel in not accomplishing my goal.

Now let's discuss the pleasure I will experience when I achieve this goal: I can see my name on Amazon, I give other people a reason to talk with me for speaking engagements and consulting assignments, I establish myself as an expert, I start making progress towards my goals of creating passive income, and I accomplish a lifelong dream.

What action will I take every day to achieve this goal? I will get up at 5:00 AM and write from 5:30 to 7:00 every weekday morning. I will reward myself by sleeping late on weekends.

I want the support of my wife. How can I enlist her help? I ask myself the following questions about how to make this happen.

What's in it for my wife?

She wants me to be happy and working on something that is important to me. She will also benefit financially after the book is published.

What is the least I will accept?

> Creating enough time in our schedules to find time to write the book.

What kinds of problems can surface?

> I will be getting up earlier than she does. I might wake her up in the morning. I need time to gather the data. This will result in time away from her (missing the time we usually spend together). The expense of publishing a book.

What are the benefits to all parties to successfully resolving those problems?

1. Waking her up in the morning - To address this problem I will buy a second alarm clock that I will keep on my side of the bed as to not to disturb my wife. I'll take my shower after she gets up in the morning. As a thank you, I'll serve her coffee in bed every morning.

2. Taking the time to gather the data and missing time we spend together - this will be accomplished by interviewing every company that submits a nomination for the conference. The interviews must be done during business hours, over the phone and when we (my wife and I) do not have a scheduled activity. We will schedule weekly dates.

3. Expense of publishing - Since it will take so long to write this I will budget funds each week to reduce the impact of getting this published.

How will I bring this process to a successful conclusion for all parties?

> Get my wife's acceptance and buy-in on the above plan. If my wife does not accept my plan, I will do the book before she gets up in the morning and after she goes to bed at night.

As you can see, using this process you will be proactive in defining obstacles that get in your way while creating win/win situations that allow you to move forward. If you cannot create a win/win situation, you will be able to identify it more quickly and know when to stop the process.

Now that you have read this, go back to the beginning of this chapter and do the exercises. This is about clarity in your life. There are no right or wrong answers. Know that what you document today will more than likely change tomorrow. As I get clearer and more focused on my desired outcomes I see possibilities I did not see yesterday. Things I documented yesterday may not be important to me tomorrow. Be flexible, persistent and focused.

CHAPTER 12:

WHAT NEXT?

"Work is good!"

–Robert Schepens

When I first started my business I had every one of the problems I discuss in this book. That is how I know about them and how to implement the necessary interventions to be successful. I could not fix them if I could not determine the problem.

Here is what I now know:

- You can't do it yourself.

- Masterminds don't work unless you have accountability built into the process.

- You need a strong facilitator to ensure no one dominates.

- You need a well defined process.

Here is what I did, and you can do the same thing.

- It had to be a living process that worked with everyone who participated.

- Everyone had to participate in each meeting and get value from it.

- It had to attract like-minded people who understood that they needed objective advice from others and were willing to share what they know with others.

- Everyone needed to be held accountable for working on what's important to them.

- It required commitment both to attend the meetings and to achieve their goals.

- It needed to drive the nine actions discussed above. It needed to enforce, encourage and allow people who participate to become selfish, take ownership, focus on results, learn how to become more effective in dealing with people, and encourage focus, discipline, persistence, ideas and action.

I created the Business Mastery Advisory Board(tm). Why is the Business Mastery Advisory Board(tm) so important? Business owners are hounded by lawyers, accountants, business coaches and other so-called experts who claim they can help solve all your business problems. It does not matter what kinds of problems: sales, marketing, customer service, finance, operations, IT, etc.; the promises are the same.

We know it is just not possible to be all things to all people. As a result, business owners do not know who to trust or where to turn for objective, effective feedback and advice. Where can a business owner go to discuss all their problems, mistakes, challenges and opportunities and get positive, constructive feedback, in a safe environment, and walk out of each meeting feeling great because they've made substantial progress?

There are not many places like that. A place that is **safe, effective, objective,** and **cost effective**. A place where business owners can grow personally and professionally, a place where they learn to think differently about their problems and realize they are not alone. A place where they can receive honest feedback that focuses on the problems that hinder their success. That is why the Business Mastery Advisory Board was created.

The essence of the Business Mastery Advisory Board is that successful people understand that multiple minds and multiple experiences are far smarter, more effective and more efficient than any single mind or experience. Simply stated, safer, more effective and better decisions are made.

This process works because the nine actions I discuss throughout this book have been isolated so each member can focus on their intelligent self-interest.

If you are going to create your own advisory board, follow these simply rules and charge something for this service. People do not value what they get for free. No active selling to other members, treat the meetings as sacred by attending them all, share what you know and be open to receiving feedback from others, no competition (you will never share your category), keep everything confidential, and commit to the group for 12 months. If you want to run one, create one, or participate in one, go to http://www.rpfgroupinc.com.

109

ADDITIONAL RESOURCES

49 Marketing Secrets (THAT WORK) to Grow Sales

You want to grow sales but you are not sure how? You know the right marketing program will take your business to the next level but you don't know who to trust? There is so much "noise" that you don't know what works? If you feel that way, you've come to the right place.

49 Marketing Secrets (that work) to Grow Sales was developed with you in mind.

Marketing: it was a marketing problem. As we discussed, the problem I've heard over and over again: I don't know what works.

- There are so many "experts" I don't know who to trust.

- It costs too much.

I went to marketing experts and asked them what they did to help their clients, and I went to business owners and asked them what they did to grow their businesses. There were four goals for the book:

- Affordable

- Only effective, PROVEN marketing methods would be included

- Include step by step instructions

- Author's contact information available so you can learn more

Here's What Other Marketing Experts Say about 49 Marketing Secrets

"The heavy hitters, the shining stars, the bright lights – they're all here for you in this brilliant and enlightening book. It should be mandatory reading for anyone who loves marketing and profits."

Jay Conrad Levinson, The Father of Guerrilla Marketing, author of the "Guerrilla Marketing" series of books with over 14 million sold; now in 43 languages

"Success in business requires a strong vision, a positive attitude and knowing what to do and when to do it. I'm astonished by how many answers this book has to the questions business owners ask all the time. Strong marketing paves the way to lasting success, and you'll find what you need in '49 Marketing Secrets' to get wherever you want to go."

Joe Vitale, author of "The Attractor Factor" and "Zero Limits"

"Wow. A wealth of info that only a fool would ignore."

Person's name, author of "Book title"[.1]

To Order this book go to www.49marketingsecrets.com

The Platinum Rule for Small Business Mastery

"This fast-moving, practical book gives you personal strategies you can use to operate more efficiently and build your business faster."

Brian Tracy, Author, "The Way to Wealth"

The Platinum Rule for Small Business Mastery will help you put "people" back into the business by learning to "treat others the way they want to be treated."

You will learn:

1. The strengths of your natural behavioral style and how to leverage them

2. To discover common traits shared by effective leaders who have mastered behavioral adaptability

3. Invaluable information about how your behavioral style can be leveraged to create an effective culture that permeates every facet of your business

4. How to create discipline within your organization that guarantees predictable results

5. How to develop a winning attitude that improves every facet of your business

6. Why your natural behavioral style may be impeding your ability to take calculated risks that are necessary to build a winning business

7. How to leverage your natural behavioral style within your particular selling environment

8. How to use psychographics in customizing your marketing messages

Franchise Opportunities

Do you want to get involved in a business model that drives these behaviors? If so, The Business Mastery Advisory Board' Franchise might be right for you.

Do you believe that multiple minds and multiple experiences are far smarter, more effective and more efficient than any single mind or experience in the decision making process? Do you want to make a difference, help change lives, and make money?

Why Do Business Owners Need a Business Mastery Advisory Board(tm)?

Each company president, CEO, and business owner interviewed discussed the importance of having trusted advisors dedicated to providing constructive feedback, practical advice, positive suggestions, and best practices that allow them to grow, flourish, and get results. Nearly all the business owners interviewed preferred a paid board of advisors to the alternatives available.

What is a Business Mastery Advisory Board(tm)?

The Business Mastery Advisory Board is a member organization dedicated to providing objective feedback, constructive advice, workable suggestions, accountability, and best practices that allow the members to grow, flourish, and get results.

If you think owning a Business Mastery Advisory Board is right for you, or you want to join one, visit our website (www.rpfgroupinc.com) to learn more.

Other Resources I Have Enjoyed

There are many great books on the market today. Below are some materials I have read or been exposed to as I have attended conferences and seminars. I am making them available if you want to learn more. Do not construe the material I have listed here as an endorsement for the concepts in this book. I found the books (material) to be interesting, informative and in some cases inspirational and I wanted to share them with you.

Intelligent Self-Interest

Virtue of Selfishness - Ayn Rand, www.aynrand.org

Atlas Shrugged - Ayn Rand, www.aynrand.org

I Learning Global - On Demand Training, www.ilearningglobal.biz/ronf

The Psychology of Achievement - Brian Tracy, www.briantracy.com

People

The Platinum Rule" - Dr. Tony Alessandra, www.alessandra.com

How to Win Friends and Influence People - Dale Carnegie, www.dalecarnegie.com

Emotional Intelligence - Daniel Goleman

Foundational Networking - Frank Agin, www.foundationalnetworking.com

Marketing

Mind Capture - Tony Rubleski - www.mindcapturegroup.com

Trade Show Profit SECRETS - Steve Underation, www. TradeShowProfitSystems.com, contact Steve at Help@ TradeShowProfitSystems.com

The Experience Economy - B. Joseph Pine II and James H. Gilmore, www. strategichorizons.com

Free Buzz Marketing Course - http://blog.buzzoodle.com

Internet Dough - Don Philabaum, http://internetdough.net

International Referral Group - Dan Minick, www.irnlink.com

B to B Connect - Laura Leggett, www.btobconnect.com

Focus

The Power of Focus - Jack Canfield, Mark Victor Hanson, Les Hewitt

Discipline

The Four Hour Work Week - Tim Ferris, www.fourhourworkweek.com

Ideas

Beyond the Power of Positive Thinking - Dr. Robert Anthony, drrobertanthony.com

Same Game New Rules, 23 Timeless Principles for Selling and Negotiating - Bill Caskey

Diffusion of Innovations - Everett Rogers

The Success Principles - Jack Canfield

Science of Mind - Ernst Holmes

About The Authors

Ron Finklestein

"Small Business Success Expert"
"Entrepreneur"
"Passionate"
"Leader"
"Motivator"
"Gets Results"

"Team Builder"

This is how business leaders and clients describe Ron.

After a successful consulting career, Ron has spent the past six years building his business, AKRIS INC, and helping entrepreneurs and business owners build their businesses by helping them solve the tough problems that hold them back. Ron is called "Your Small Business Success Expert" by his clients because of his passion for their success and his knowledge of business. Ron is passionate about making a difference in people's lives by helping them to achieve their business and personal goals and dreams.

Ron has experience in working with businesses across a wide range of industries and on every aspect of a business, from information technology to marketing, leadership to sales, allowing him to offer practical and proven ideas and strategies to improve any business. Ron knows and understands that all successful people exhibit nine actions and he has built products to help implement these actions in businesses of all sizes. Because of the depth and breadth of Ron's experience, he can quickly and decisively see and identify business and personal challenges, identify innovative solutions, and create opportunities out of most any problem.

Ron has an established reputation for building strong relationships and using those relationships to help others enhance their own personal and professional success. Ron is a frequent speaker and presenter on various business topics including *Building Businesses, Leadership,* The Platinum Rule®, *Attitudes and Actions of Success, Sales and Marketing,*

Entrepreneurship, Business Strategies and Business Mastery. Ron is involved with numerous business, non-profit organizations and initiatives as part of his personal commitment to personal and professional growth and the growth of his clients.

Ron has owned his business, AKRIS INC, since 2002. AKRIS INC focuses on helping grow and improve small businesses.

- Twenty-five years of Fortune 1000 consulting experience

- Author of Celebrating Success! 14 Ways to Create a Successful Company (http://www.yourbusinesscoach.net). This is a study of small businesses and what they do to be successful.

- Ron is also co-author of The Platinum Rule for Small Business Mastery with Dr. Tony Alessandra and Scott Zimmerman. This book helps you understand how to get the best from the employees in your organization.

- Owner of AKRIS INC, (www.akris.net) which provides business coaching and consulting services to business owners and entrepreneurs to help them build a better business.

- Creator of The RPF GROUP INC Business Mastery Advisory Board and the associated franchise program (http://www.rpfgroupinc.com). The Business Mastery Advisory Board allows business owners to learn, grow and prosper by understanding that multiple minds are more effective in making effective decisions than any single mind.

Currently, Ron resides in Akron, Ohio, where he is president of AKRIS INC. He spends his time consulting, coaching small business owners to greater success, and writing and speaking about how to implement success strategies in business.

Over the years Ron has spoken to or for business groups, chambers of commerce, community groups, associations, in-house training programs, continuing education programs, seminars, lunch and learns, workshops, etc. Participants and attendees have described Ron as "energizing," "enthusiastic," "fun," "engaging," "motivational," "thoughtful," "informative," "inspiring," "effective," and "motivating." If you are interested in learning how Ron can help you in your business or in having Ron speak to your business, team, organization, association or group, contact him at (330) 990-0788 or ron@akris.net / www.rpfgroupinc.com.

Current Seminars and Workshops Include:

1. Dealing with difficult people

2. Building Better Relationships using The Platinum Rule

3. A variety of Sales and Marketing programs (based on his books)

4. Attitudes and Actions of Success/Overcoming Adversity

Consulting Programs

1. Publishing your non-fiction book

2. Individual Coaching / Group Coaching

3. Business Mastery Advisory Board

Key Note Speeches

Ron will create a custom speech designed specifically for your audience. The content comes from his four books and his many years of real life experience working in the trenches. His books include: The Platinum Rule for Small Business Mastery, Celebrating Success! Fourteen Ways to Create a Successful Company, 49 Marketing Secrets (THAT WORK) to Grow Sales and Learning to Think Differently.

Robert A. Schepens

Robert is the President/ Owner of Champion Personnel System, Inc of North East Ohio, a flexible staffing company with 6 offices and 45 years of exceptional service to Northeast Ohio. Mr. Schepens acquired the company from his father in 1995 and through defining a clear vision built a multiple-office company that has achieved: Top 10 Most Dependable Staffing Services in Central USA (Fortune Magazine April 2008), ISO 9001:2000 Certified, a two-time Weatherhead 100 Fastest Growing Privately Held Company Award Winner, a two-time Northcoast 99 Best Companies to Work For in Northeast Ohio award winner, The First Drug Free Staffing Service Workplace Level II OBWC Certified company in Ohio, and Winner of the Northeast Ohio Business Success Award.

Mr. Schepens is also Principle Founder and CEO of A Job Near Home.com, a TREEN ™, Tool for Regional Employment and Economic Networking for Northeast Ohio, and the President of Drug Free Solutions NEO, a drug testing and drug-free workplace training and consulting corporation. Robert hosts 3 Video channels on A Job Near Home.com: "E2e" (Entrepreneur to entrepreneur) showcasing the most successful Entrepreneurs in Northeast Ohio, "People Making A Difference in NEO" (PMAD), highlighting Social Entrepreneurs and their positive impact on the region, and "Innovation NEO", that focuses on the people and organizations leading the way to the future in Northeast Ohio.

Mr. Schepens serves on the Friends of Entrepreneur Preparatory School Board of Directors and is an active volunteer in the community of Northeast Ohio. He is a graduate of Valparaiso University and attended Fitzwilliam College, Cambridge University in England. He can be reached at: ras@ajobnearhhome.com